OUR LIFE
INTERRUPTED

And the Prayers That Brought Us Through

CONDASE WEEKES-BEST

True Short Stories of Challenges and Triumphs
and the Prayers That Brought Us Through

ISBN 978-1-0980-3131-2 (paperback)
ISBN 978-1-0980-4330-8 (hardcover)
ISBN 978-1-0980-3132-9 (digital)

Christian Faith Publishing, Inc.
832 Park Avenue
Meadville, PA 16335
www.christianfaithpublishing.com

Scripture quotations are taken from THE HOLY BIBLE, NEW INTERNATIONAL VERSION®, NIV® Copyright © 1973, 1978, 1984, 2011 by Biblica, Inc.™ Used by permission. All rights reserved worldwide.

Printed in the United States of America

ACKNOWLEDGEMENTS

I would like to acknowledge my Heavenly Father. I simply love Him and continue to seek Him in all that I do. I pray that this work of testimonies would bring praise, glory, and honor to His name.

I would also like to thank my husband Danny for the depth of his love, his strength, and his wisdom. I firmly believe that every woman should marry their best friend, and I am grateful to God that I married mine. Danny, for your unwavering love, encouragement, and support, I will be forever indebted to you. My children, Tyler and Miles Jeremiah, have been my biggest cheerleaders and two of the most influential people in my life. My prayer is that my sons will know God intimately and know that He will not fail.

Special thanks to my mothers. My birth mother, Lillian, for introducing God to me at an early age. My mother-in-law, Harriet, for being a real example of living by faith. You both continue to challenge me to rise above the challenges of life; by your faith, prayers, intellect, determination, and wisdom.

To my sisters, some of the most honest and loyal sister-friends that I know. Maria, Danielle, and Pamela. None of us would want to revisit the year 2013. There were months and moments that it seemed we would not make it out alive during that year. Our families experienced severe difficulties. Our journeys may have had different paths, but we all needed, depended, and leaned on each other throughout these tumultuous years. You each walked beside me without judgment, and there were times that it was your faith that supported me. These times would have been so much more difficult without your guidance, support, and strength. Thank you.

Special love and thanks to the new additions in my life, for the seasons that you entered, and the impact that you are making—ALL things are possible when we believe.

CONTENTS

Dear Readers,

With deep gratitude and humility, I say thank you for choosing to purchase and read this book. This book will travel to places that I may never go, and touch lives that I may never personally meet. My prayer and hope are that these true short stories and prayers will be a blessing and a challenge to you.

My intent is for these stories to convey messages of hope, faith, and love. That each reader would be strengthened and be full of confidence in God's ability to be our shelter in the time of storm. That each reader would rely entirely on God's ability to be our help in times of trouble and our hope when it seems all hope is gone.

I convey the challenges, trials, and tests that my family has gone through with these stories. But they also tell how God always magnified himself on our behalf, giving us the victory again and again.

Happy reading!

CHAPTER 1

MY STEWARDSHIP PRAYER

Father, you are the Giver of gifts, talents, and abilities. Today I come before you and I surrender my gifts, talents, and abilities to you. I repent for those times and instances where I became like the servant in the Bible, (Matthew 25:18) who was given one talent and chose not to utilize it. His attitude was one of careless ungratefulness. Instead of using his one talent as an investment tool, he foolishly buried it and then turned around and blamed You for his selfish act. Father, I do not want to behave in this way. I am sorry for those instances where I looked at my one talent as insufficient and meaningless. Forgive me for my self-righteous attitude and for the spirit of laziness and procrastination that caused me to lack vision, insight, and wisdom.

Today, I declare that I will use every gift and talent for your glory and praise. I give you back each ability and I thank you for the wisdom to manage them well. I thank you for the double portion that is upon every talent and gift in my life. I thank you for understanding me and knowing the capabilities you have given me. You know me so well that you understand why you blessed me with the talents that you gave me. I desire to hear you say, "Well done, my good and faithful servant." I will no longer hide my talents, neither will I curse you, in my heart. I will submit my talents to you and allow your wisdom to guide me forward in using them for your glory, in Jesus Name I pray. Amen.

THE BEGINNING

The stories and testimonies that I share are mostly from the years 2013 through 2018; however, there may be times, I will go further back so that you can understand the depth of the circumstances and the challenges. In my story, *Our Life Interrupted,* I have compiled a series of situations in our lives where our complete trust and confidence in God was an absolute necessity. These situations took place over five years and could have been crippling, if not for the hands of God upon my life, my home, my family, and my marriage.

I wrote this book to inspire, challenge, prune, and prepare you for God's will and purpose to be done in your life. I will start at the place where it all began.

I was born and raised on the small, not well-known island of Montserrat, British West Indies. A tiny thirty-nine and one half square miles island, about fifteen minutes away from Antigua by plane, one hour by boat. Montserrat, a small hidden gem in the Caribbean, is a tropical paradise. Well-known independent islands such as St.Kitts & Nevis and Antigua & Barbuda with international airports and aggressive tourist marketing agendas surround Montserrat. Montserrat is known as the Emerald Isle of the Caribbean. One of a handful of Caribbean Islands that remains under British rule.

Imagine a small island nestled in the warm waters of the Caribbean Sea. This Eden-like paradise is surrounded by beaches that boast rich volcanic black sand. The sand becomes blistering hot during the day because of the tropical weather that the island enjoys year-round. The landscape is vibrant and colorful. The mountains stand tall and proud. As far as the eye can see, there is a rich, lush, and green scenery covering the land. Montserrat enjoys a mountainous terrain, with winding roads, very steep hills, and deep valleys, which makes driving on the left side of the road somewhat challenging for tourists.

Daybreak was and is still my favorite time of day. Daybreak on the island is like an orchestra and nighttime like a choir. Before daybreak each day, one would wake to the sounds of roosters crowing. Their loud cries would be the first alarm clock across the island, informing everyone that another day has begun. Not long after, the goats, sheep, cows, donkeys, turkeys would remind us that the time for sleep is over. Morning would begin, and one would hear praying, singing, or conversations coming from homes or people walking on the streets. Another day had begun!

The island would come alive with familiar sounds. The truck that carried the local village men who worked with the government public works could be heard squeaking at different stops. People were heard laughing and speaking loudly in the local patois. The school buses would rush up the hill to collect school children heading off to the high schools. Sprinkled around different parts of the village, school children wearing different uniforms that identified which school students attended were seen talking and waiting around for the school buses. The hustle and bustle of the day would begin, yet everyone moved at an island pace. There was no urgency to get anywhere immediately. Neighbors greeted each other, sometimes stopping to inquire about an elderly loved one, someone who was sick, or simply touching base. We looked out for each other, showing compassion and concern.

As the day started peacefully, so it ended. Families sat outside on their verandas talking and laughing, their voices carried by the wind. Neighbors passed by greeting each other, spending time to catch up on the day's news. As dusk settled across the island, one could hear the radio broadcaster's animated voice reading the local news, followed by news from the British Broadcasting Company (BBC). As it got darker, people moved inside their homes, and lights flickered on. As darkness settled in, Crickets began to chirp, dogs began to bark, frogs would began to sing as another day closes. Everyone settled in for another restful night.

We enjoyed wide variety of seasonal fruits and vegetables. Our rich volcanic soil assists in the overproduction of food. In the mango season, the mango trees would be pregnant with mangoes. We had many different variations of mangoes. The same is true for any season and the fruits or vegetables that that specific season produced. We have mangoes, bananas, tamarinds, sugar apples, breadfruits, and many other types of fruits and vegetables. Indeed, this land is blessed by God.

Montserrat is an English-speaking island with a local patois that is spoken across the island community. When I was growing up, Montserrat had a population of 12,000 people. We have a strong Irish heritage due to the Irish, who first arrived in Montserrat in 1632. We are the only island in the Caribbean that celebrates St. Patrick Day, with a full week of celebrations and festivities. This celebration is a shared bond that connects us to our Irish heritage. Montserratians are strong, independent, talented, and courageous people who are warm, open, and exceptionally friendly. In this community, it was indeed the village that raised each child—this was not just an African proverb. We were disciplined at home, school, and from village to village. And within this small island community, the seniors took their role to introduce every child to God extremely seriously. This community, with firm faith in God and strong family relationships, developed and instilled my values. This was the island home that taught me right from wrong and gave me the courage to fly no matter how gray the skies looked. I grew up in this cocoon, where I was sheltered, protected, pruned, and prepared for the world.

From my earliest memory, the mothers, grandmothers, and great-grandmothers that I grew up with had a stable relationship with God. It did not matter what ministry they fellowshipped; everything they did came from a deep reverence for God. They were the standard bearers, and passing the spiritual torch to those who came after them, was extremely important. Their Christian life impacted everything we did. Looking back, we did not have much in the way of material things, but we had a strong community. We were rich in love, respect, honor, and our love for God. The island raised every child, and love for God was taught right out of the womb. We were taught at home, at school, and at church. On Montserrat, there was no separation of church and state. It was common for us as children growing up in this community to attend church services six days a week and on Sundays three times a day. Yes! In this small island, God was indeed the front, back, and center of our lives. This love and honor for God was passed onto us. The mothers ensured that they left a strong spiritual legacy for the generations to come. I remember attending all-day shut-in prayer services with the mothers of the church. For they took God at his Word that declares in Proverbs 22:6, *"Train up a child in the way that they should go, and when they are old they will not depart from it."* This upbringing shaped me, and from this foundation, I learned morals and values. But more than anything, my young and tender heart got to learn of the Living God. I did not know it then, but my childhood upbringing was going to shape my adult life in so many ways.

My mother, whom I love deeply, had a challenging life! My mother Lillian, or "Clarie" as she was commonly known on the island, is an inspiring woman. She was born and raised on the island of Montserrat in the late 1940s to a single parent. This was a tumultuous time to be born in the Caribbean. Montserrat was part of the British Federal Colony of the Leeward Islands. It was during this time that Montserratians were given the right to vote. It was also during this era that Montserrat became a colony. My mother grew up in this period, perhaps not understanding the significance of what was taking place around her. Montserrat was changing because the world was changing. At the age of thirteen, my mother suffered a severe loss. Her mother, Anne who was only 33 years old, died suddenly from fibroids. My grandmother did not receive the medical help that may have saved her life. My grandmother's death left an enormous void in my mother's life. My brothers and I felt that loss through the years. We did not have the honor of knowing our grandmother, and she did not have the privilege of knowing us. I cannot imagine the devastation my mother endured; she was an orphan. Her father was alive but did not acknowledge her as his daughter. My great-grandmother, fondly called Daiday continued with the raising of my mother. Her real name was Rhoda, but as is common on the island, everyone has a formal name but was assigned a nickname that stuck. With my great-grandmother's help and influence, my brothers Isaac (known as Eddie), and Randolph and myself were introduced to the Living God at a very early age. If my mother was passionate about God, my great-grandmother was even more so.

Daiday played an important role within the ministry even before I was born. In those days, there was no electricity on the island. My great-grandmother had the responsibility of ensuring that the lamp used for the ministry was always well-maintained. By that, I mean clean, with the right amount of oil, and ready to be lit for services. My great-grandmother served as the church administrator as well as the church treasurer. She passed away in the early eighties when I was thirteen, but the memories I have of her standing against the front door knocking in tune to one of the old songs of Zion remains strongly sketched in my memory.

My mother is a source of strength. I cannot fathom the inner strength, courage, wisdom, and fortitude that she had as a young, naïve mother. As a young innocent teenager, she had three children. My mom had her first child at fifteen, second at sixteen, and me at twenty. My mother built a stable and secure life for us. Any woman having three children out of wedlock in the 1960s in such a small island community endured paralyzing shame. People may have considered my mom a loose woman, not understanding the depth of what she had to overcome as a teenage girl without parents to protect her. Imagine the words used to describe her and the shame that she encountered. I cannot fathom that her community realized that she was an open target and a prey because she was an orphan.

My mom is a woman who endured and experienced poverty, rejection, and humiliation. But she never wavered in her faith in God. She served God, instilling His laws and values into our lives. My mother continued to help and support others even in times of significant need. My mom aspired to become better than the critics and skeptics who insisted that she would not amount to much. At times, even those who attend ministries to worship the Lord sometimes condemn and ridicule others. They hold themselves higher and think of themselves as better than others. There is such a story in the Bible of the woman caught in adultery. This is found in John 8:1–11. This adulterous woman was already condemned and almost ready to be put to death, but Jesus in His infinite wisdom, full of grace and compassion said to her accusers "Let he who is without sin cast the first stone." After Jesus made this statement, all of her accusers walked away. My mother insists that with God, even the impossible becomes possible.

My mother always aspired to be better, and this became the mantra for us. She inspired us to dream and to dream big. Mom did not finish her education, so our education was her priority. She instilled in us this deep need to work hard and do our best. And everything that she did, all the decisions she made, she peppered them with much prayer. We grew up with our mother, we were a team, and each team member had a say in what the team did. But the one thing that she did not invite our comments, suggestions, and feelings about was our church life. It was merely an understanding that there will be no tolerance for not going to church. I remember daily waking before daybreak to hearing my mother crying out to God in prayer. A practice my family now hears from me. She not only sent us to church, but she also lived the life within our home.

In the late '80s my mother decided we should move to the United States. There she was dreaming again! Mom told us that moving to America would benefit our education and provide opportunities that we would not have in Montserrat. Of course, at the age of fifteen, I did not understand the desire to uproot what I thought was a secure family life, to start over in America. I loved my life on the island and wanted to remain in my bubble. Also, only my mother had legal documents to travel to the United States. My brothers and I would have to go through the application process, which was often lengthy. That minute detail did not prevent my mother from planning and moving forward. For she lived a life of faith, and she believed that faith without action is dead.

Before our family moved to Boston, my mother spent the next two to three years living in Puerto Rico, six months, as her visa allowed. I was left with my two older brothers, Eddie and Randolph, and had the responsibility of managing and maintaining our home. Although Mom was in Puerto Rico for months at a time, we felt her presence at home. We were and still are a close-knitted family. Perhaps this was because my mom and all three of us grew up together. Whenever my mom made a decision, we knew the reasons, the boundaries, our roles, and the expectations. Staying with my older brothers was never an issue for me, for my mother had already set the expectations. She always kept in touch. We understood the purpose for her absence and wanted her to succeed, which meant that everyone had to do their part. My mother's decision helped us, and benefited extended family in our community. During those years, she regularly sent home barrels with food and clothes. These barrels of food items provided for many of us.

In our home, attending church was mandatory, but, there was no pressure to have an intimate relationship with God. Our community believed if we were around God, He would meet us at the appointed time. We attended church services whenever the doors opened. We attended ministry services with a limited wardrobe and the right attitude. My siblings and I dutifully obeyed. It was important to mom to pass on her love for God to us. My mom believes that God will protect and provide for us, as He did for her as a teenage mother, and continues even today.

It was during one of her absences that I seriously gave my life to the Lord. It was a revival in another village, and I remembered the peace and freedom I felt after committing my life to Christ. After accepting Christ into my life, I had the responsibility of being the youth leader and sunday school teacher in my local church. I performed these assignments in earnest through the lenses and with the innocence of a teenager.

CHAPTER 2

MY THANKSGIVING PRAYER

Thank you Father for your deep love for me. Thank you for your faithful kindness to me. Thank you for tenderly and lovingly watching over me. Thank you for guiding and guarding my steps, especially in those times when I was in the wrong places at the wrong times. Thank you that you know the plans you have for me and that these plans you have written in my DNA are good. Thank you for choosing me, although I did not yet know You. Father, like the story of King Cyrus found in Isaiah 45, You my Heavenly Father had already prophesied of the great things that You have called me to do.

Thank you Father for going before me and leveling the mountains. Thank you for smashing down gates of bronze and cutting through bars of iron on my behalf. Thank you for giving me treasures hidden in the darkness. Yes! secret riches will be given to me in this hour. Thank you that you called me for this work even when I did not know you. Thank you for equipping me for battle, so all the world will know there is no other God. This is the Word of the Lord concerning me, in Jesus name. Amen (Isaiah 45).

Conversation between Heavenly Father and myself:
Heavenly Father: "Condase, do you trust me?"
Condase: "I do, Father!"
Heavenly Father: "Do you really trust me?
Condase: I do.
Heavenly Father: Watch and see what I will do for you, for you are my beloved daughter in whom I delight. My daughter, I will not allow you to be put to shame. No, you will not be an

object of mockery. The enemy will not laugh at you. I know that the walls seem to be closing in but look to me. I got you, and I've got this. Trust me. I will not let you fail."

Thank you Father for not allowing me to fail. Thank you for going beside me, yet you are around me like a shield. Truly there is no god like you. I love and appreciate you, in Jesus name. Amen.

A RUDE AWAKENING

I migrated to the United States in the summer of 1988 with my older brother Eddie after I completed high school. As a young teenage girl from a tiny island where you knew everyone, and everyone knew you, this was a challenging transition for me. I had to learn and adapt quickly, for life in America was entirely different from life on a small island. The atmosphere was stifling. So many people, so many cars, and everyone always in a hurry. No one greeted you! It seemed almost as I was invisible. I was used to the weather being either rain or sunshine, but I had to become used to other seasons, including winter, which to me was a blistering cold season.

I felt isolated, and as soon as I spoke, everyone asked about my accent, as if I came from Mars. I was just one of many people hustling to and fro. When I took the bus, no one knew my name, and no one was interested in getting to know me. My family sternly cautioned me against speaking with strangers, continually reminding me that we were no longer in our close-knitted, friendly island community. Back home, I was always outside involved in some vigorous outdoor activity, such as cricket, jump-rope, dodgeball, hide-and-seek, or any other games that we designed as children. The adjustments I made to be always on guard was tiring and frustrating. Adapting to this new lifestyle was difficult.

In Montserrat, we owned our own house. We had a yard, garden, and animals. I knew all the people in my village, and I never lacked someone to play or visit. I had a busy social life in Montserrat. Now I was stuck in an apartment with other people living on different floors, and we had to pay rent. Did we leave our peaceful, idyllic life for better opportunities in this place? I was not convinced that my mother made the best decision.

I missed my friends. Some of my family and friends that migrated before me had grown up and changed and, even to them, I seemed uncultured. They had become Americanized. I was homesick for a long time. My immediate family surrounded me, which was my only saving grace. There was nothing to do and nowhere to go. My mother, who I was used to seeing every day when we were in Montserrat, now had a live-in job. She did not return home to the apartment until Friday evenings. I was a prisoner in the apartment until the weekends, then we were able to go shopping and attend ministry on Sundays. I was excited about the social aspects of attending ministry. I was excited to make new friends but the young people treated me unkindly. In my new life in America, I watched television for hours, unlike Montserrat where we watched television in limited time-periods during the evenings. Food was affordable and plentiful, but I missed the fresh organic foods of my home. I would have traded all of this for a one-way ticket back to Montserrat. I endured the process, but I certainly did not enjoy it.

I was not allowed to call my friends in Montserrat because calls were costly. When I disobeyed, I got in serious trouble. I was unable to work because I had no legal documents. I had no money because I could not work. I was in a stuck situation, and I dreamt of a time when I could move beyond what I was going through. The changing seasons were the worst experiences for me, especially the dark, long, and cold winter months. My first winter is still a memory that haunts me. My first winter was a chilling reality for several reasons. Waking up in Montserrat, a sunny bright day meant it was another hot, ninety-five degrees day. In this consistently tropical weather, the sky was cloudless, with lots of wind in the shade. My first experience of winter, I was fooled by the sunny bright days, thinking that they were similar to my home in Montserrat. I ventured outside inappropriately dressed in my summer clothes, not realizing the bitter coldness of the New England winters. One memory was leaving classes and waiting at the bus stop. It was freezing cold. My eyes were watering, my teeth were chattering, my fingers and toes were frostbitten. The coldness seeped into my bones. I was not wearing a hat, or gloves, and I did not have a winter wardrobe. No one instructed me that the change of seasons meant changes in my entire wardrobe. Back home, we wore summer clothes all year round, with perhaps the addition of sweaters in the rainy season. I learned quickly and made the adjustments needed.

Over time, I made the necessary changes and soon adjusted to my new home. During my settling-in period and because education was so important to my mother, I got accepted and attended community college. My acceptance to college presented its challenges, as I attended as an international student. International students pay higher tuition than if one was a resident of the state. Financially, it was difficult. Time and time again, I overcame barriers and hurdles. However, with my mother's fierce determination and my hard work, I persevered and graduated from a community college after two years with an Associate Degree in English.

Spiritually, my life changed. God was no longer my focus. I was not committed to Him as I used to be. I was distracted. I started to hang out with my college friends, mostly from the islands. Many of them knew of God but had no real relationship with Him. And after many seasons of being lukewarm, I eventually became spiritually cold. I would still attend ministry, but I had lost my love, zeal, and fire for God. I had so many examples of God's grace and love, was now living a life that totally ignored His presence. In my effort to fit in, I found myself going to parties, to dance clubs, and behaving in ways that did not honor God. The question always lingered in my heart, "What if the rapture were to take place now, where would I spend eternity?" I was too stubborn and proud to answer the question.

Eventually, I backslid. I was in my twenties and lured into the lie that I needed to live my life because I was only young once. But I thank God for His faithfulness. After graduating from community college, I continued to pursue my education at a four-year institution. The cost to attend was extremely expensive as I was still paying tuition as an international student. After two semesters, it became apparent that the cost of continuing college as an international student was a steep financial burden my family could no longer afford. I walked away from college with the intent that someday I would complete my education. Today I have a Master's degree in Business Administration.

I did not have the legal documents needed to obtain lawful employment. Not having legal documents was a severe test, as I was unable to work toward the goals that I wanted to achieve. Even though I always thought of returning home, I did not want to return home without being able to return to the United States. That would be shameful. The constant worry of being stuck was always at the forefront of my mind. Through the connections at the ministry, I secured employment at a local retail store. I was a good, hardworking employee, well-liked by the managers. I worked as a cashier, stocked the shelves, and was eventually given additional responsibilities in the office. I started to balance the cash registers, completed paperwork and managing the scheduling of employees. One day, my manager informed that I could no longer work there. Upper management discovered that I did not have legal documentation. My manager had no other choice but to terminate my employment. I was disappointed and humiliated.

I ended up working in a nursing home for seniors. The owner hired me to clean, assist with meal preparation, and help the residents of the facility when needed. I was making the best of what I thought was a bad situation, for this was not how I envisioned my late teens. Things were bad and I desperately needed a breakthrough, yet I still did not turn to God. I kept on trying to walk in my own understanding. My father, whom I met at the age of eighteen, was an American citizen. He decided to file for me to obtain legal documents. I was waiting on my documentation to be processed, but I did not have a time frame to measure the process. This wait seemed long, and I had grown tired and weary in my waiting. I was stuck! I could not move forward, and this was extremely frustrating to me.

After four years, I received the documents that made me eligible to live and work in the United States. Today as I write, I am a United States citizen. I will never forget these experiences. I remember the feelings of isolation, anger, and desperation that I went through.

These experiences allow me to completely relate to the uncertainty, frustration, and anxiety of living in America without proper documentation.

It is important that I share my early years in America with you, for there may be some reading this book in situations that seems as if God has forgotten you. You may have started to believe that you are not worth loving. Day to day living has become difficult, and dying may seem so much better than living in this moment. I encourage you to go through the pain, and the shame. I can assure you that better days are ahead. For after one season in our life comes another. Trouble comes into our lives, but trouble does not stay forever. I remind you today that even though you may have given up on yourself, even though it seems hopeless, God will never, ever give up on you. You are always His priority and the apple of His eye.

After the excitement of receiving my documentation, I actively started to look for other employment. I was still working at the nursing home, but I had already decided that this job would not be my path forward. The new challenge for me was that I had limited work experience and education. I looked for a job for many months, but it was tough. I cannot recall how many interviews I had, but there were many. Obtaining an interview was simpler than getting a job. One of the things that stood out to me was the issue of race. Ninety-nine percent of the interviewers were mostly male and white. I had to make another adjustment engaging in this diverse and complex environment culturally and mentally. I wanted to work in a bank, but every door that I walked through was closed. I persisted, sending out many resumes, but nothing seemed to be happening for me. But God always has a plan; even when we are not thinking of Him, He is always thinking of us.

One day, I saw an ad in the paper that a local bank was looking for tellers. I immediately applied. I remained hopeful that this was the opportunity that I needed to catapult me into full-time employment and eventually a career path. The year was 1993 and communication was not as instant as it is today. I remember going to work at the nursing home and calling the recruiter up to seven times a day, leaving messages about my resume and application. I was desperate.

It seemed like getting a response took forever, but after about two weeks of my aggressive, "I need a job," campaign, I received a call inviting me for an interview. I was nervous and excited!

The day of the interview finally arrived, and I felt that this was the beginning of something new. Little did I know that God had a bigger and better plan for my life. I met the interviewer and he was a young black professional. I was shocked. In my many interviews, this was the first time that I met someone who looked like me. I had an excellent interview. I was offered and accepted a job as a teller for a local bank. However, the interviewer not only gave me an opportunity but turned out to be my blessing in disguise. After years and months of delays and setbacks, God set me up! What an amazing and kind Heavenly Father. The interviewer, Danny, and I got married three years later, and we have been together for twenty-six years. We have been married for twenty-three of those years.

These are some of the miraculous ways that God worked in my life. When God has a purpose, He will continue to manifest and fulfill his plan no matter what the situation. I was not aware in those early stages that my life is purposeful. Today more than ever, I can see the will and plan of God for my life manifesting as I continue to submit and surrender to Him. Before Danny and I got married, I told God if he allowed me to marry Danny, I would completely surrender my life to Him. God honored my request, and I willingly submitted my life fully and totally to him.

I did not understand the cost of submission. One of my sister-friends and I often say that if we knew what our yes would cost, the things that we had to go through and the situations we had to endure, we may have hesitated. But thanks be to God that even though He processes us, Our Father is wise, gentle, and patient with us. Our challenge is our willingness to trust God in and through every moment of the process. For His word declares in Job 23:10, "And when he has tried me, I shall come forth as pure gold."

Gold found in the earth's depth must endure an intense process before we can enjoy its' beauty. There is the mining, separation, filtering, grinding, and smelting, which all have different levels of intensity and stages. Yet each step of the process is equally important, painful, and necessary. The ultimate purpose is to get the true beauty of that piece of gold to be beautifully displayed. When we say yes, there is a process of refining that we must go through. I did not know that challenging times were ahead, but God is always in control. Nothing and no one escapes Him, and His Word is firm and stedfast. I did not understand the process, and although there were and are seasons of severe challenges, my answer today is still yes Lord.

God processes us using different methods. God may use loss and despair, financial hardships, suffering, or whatever He chooses to develop our trust and confidence in Him. God is wise. He knows each of us intimately and fine-tunes us differently. Gold made pure in fire is an example of how God uses hardships to refine us for His purpose for our lives. Job 23:13 declares, *"yet He knows the way that I take; when He has tested me, I will come forth as gold."* God allowed Job to be tested on every level. Job lost his wealth, his children, his wife, and his reputation in one day. Job endured it all. His faith became weak, and he questioned his walk with God, but Job never walked away from God.

You may be in the fire of a challenge at this moment. Your faith may be weak. You may be weary and tired from the heat and intensity of the fire. I remind you that God is behind the scenes of this fiery challenge, pruning and preparing you for a greater purpose. Stay in the fire! You will come forth with a testimony. You will come out stronger. You will come out of the fire transformed. When we endure struggles and painful challenges, we are in the furnace of suffering. These are not enjoyable seasons or situations. We are uncomfortable, and we hurt. Rest assured that God uses these to bring us into our purpose, giving Him glory, honor, and praise.

One of the things that we fail to understand is that the book of our lives is written by God, even before He places us in our mother's womb. None of us are in this world by chance. God writes into the fiber of our DNA a mighty destiny, which we are sent to earth to fulfill. We are not accidents, and our mothers' could not abort us. God purposed in His heart that we need to be on the earth. Our time on the earth is important and what we do with the time allotted to us, matters. We are God's children who are deeply loved by Him. The seasons of pain and disappointment we encounter are already known to God, for our steps are ordered by Him. We tend to dismiss and hide the paths that cause us brokenness because they sometimes are attached to shame, anger, and pain. God divinely orchestrates our brokenness and broken moments. Our purpose is birthed out of our pain.

In this union, God blessed us with two sons, Tyler-Jace and Miles-Jeremiah, and for these blessings, I am forever grateful. Danny and I were on great career paths, with big dreams and a healthy family. We were well on our way to fulfilling the American dream.

CHAPTER 3

MY PRAYER OF TRUST AND COMPLETE CONFIDENCE IN GOD

"I will lift up my eyes to the hills, from when comes my help? My help comes from the Lord, the maker of heaven and earth." (Psalms 121:1)

Father, today I bless your name. From the rising of the sun until the going down of the same, your name is worthy to be praised. Today, I do not even know how I feel. I understand that my emotions should not dictate who You are to me. I think about the situation with my son, Miles, a child you have gifted to me. I am discouraged and disheartened. According to Your Word in Psalms 56:3, *"When I am afraid I will put my trust in thee."* Today, Father, despite how I feel, I will trust You. I bind and rebuke every spirit of fear. I bind and rebuke every evil tree planted and every evil foundation consecrated on the behalf of my family.

Father, I decree and declare, for your Word says, that I will decree a thing and it shall come to pass. I decree that the Lord of Hosts fight against those who fight against me. I speak your Word, which is alive and activated in the atmosphere, *"I am persuaded that neither death, nor life, nor angels, nor principalities, nor powers, nor things to come, neither height nor debt, nor anything else in creation, will be able to separate us from the love of God that is in Christ Jesus our Lord"* (Romans 8:38–39).

Today Father, I confess your word in 2 Corinthians 12:9 that declares *"your grace is sufficient for me."* Paul gave a vivid example of his suffering and declared even in his suffering, in his weaknesses, even when insults came, hardships, persecutions, and troubles that he suffered for Christ, Paul declared, *"For when I am weak, then I am strong" (2 Corinthians 12:10).* Father, you see me, you know me, you understand what I am dealing with better than myself. I need you in my life. I do not understand, but I recognize that this battle is not mine it is yours. So today, I pray your word in Psalms 55:1–3, *"Listen to my prayer, O God. Do not ignore my cry for help! Please listen and answer me, for I am overwhelmed by my troubles. My enemies shout at me, making loud and wicked threats. They bring trouble on me and angrily hunt me down."*

Father, in the name of Jesus, confuse them, Lord, and frustrate their plans. I see violence and conflict in the city. Father, I am glad that You are El ROI, the God who Sees. You see those who plan evil against me. I did them good, but they plot evil against me. Father, I pray that You deal with them. I give You my relationships. I ask You in the name of Jesus to separate me from those whose intents are evil. Father, in the name of Jesus, I give You every interaction, and every connection. I ask that every interaction is divinely orchestrated, and every connection is a divine connection.

Father, in the name of Jesus, I trust You with my friends and my relationships. I release them into your hands in Jesus's name. Amen. Father, I call You my Redeemer. I bless You for being my Redeemer. I am reminded of Ruth and Boaz story and how willingly and obediently Ruth sat at Boaz's feet. Ruth said without even opening her mouth, I submit to your authority. Ruth said to Boaz even in her silence, I honor you, and trust your leadership. Father, today like Ruth I come, I recognize my inadequacies, and I acknowledge my helpless hopelessness without You. So today, I simply lay at your feet. I wait for your direction and your instructions. I am so very desperate for your intervention in my life.

I surrender. I am but nothing. I give You every battle; my pain, bruises, dreams, and losses. I place them on your altar. Today, do a new thing in me. Give me a fresh anointing, a fresh outpouring of your spirit. I thank You for breaking yokes and chains in my life. I cry out Lord, asking you to sever Miles from generational and bloodline curses holding him in bondage. I plea the Blood of Jesus over Miles, over my home over my family. Father, by faith, I mark my doorpost with the Blood of Jesus, and I declare your word that when You see the Blood of Jesus You will pass over me.

Father, I declare there is no power in heaven, on the earth, under the earth, and in the sea that is greater than the power of the Living God. So today, infuse me with your power that I may do those things that glorify You in Jesus Name. Father, I ask You in Jesus name that You break the cords of bondage. Remove the rope of the oppressor, and let your glory be seen in Jesus Name. Today, I ask in Jesus Name that your will be done. I bless You and praise You for victory over defeat, and I declare that I walk in victory in Jesus name. Amen.

DELAYED OBEDIENCE
HAS CONSEQUENCES

I rededicated my life to God after my marriage. I knew this time around, I was going to give it everything within me. This walk with God was going to be all or nothing. I did not want religion, but desired relationship. I wanted to be, and still do, a friend and servant of God. I rejected the false narrative that just knowing God was sufficient. I rejected the false narrative that going to church was enough. I often pondered the stories of the great men and women of God in the Bible, wondering what made them different from myself. I wanted to know God as Moses did, like the men and women in the Bible did. I longed with everything in my heart to pursue God. Paul and Silas were prisoners, but as they worshipped God at midnight, they were delivered. I made the decision that I was going to start praying at midnight. So even though I was working in corporate America at the time, with two toddlers, my hunger for God was so strong that it led me to start praying from midnight to daybreak. To others, it may have seemed that I was going crazy, but to me, I wanted God more than anything. I wanted to experience God and serve Him with all my heart, strength, and soul.

How often in our lives have we carved out our path forward, not inviting God to have any say in the matter? I raise my hands for I am guilty. God is intentional about each of us. We are on the earth to complete a specific purpose; before we are formed in our mother's womb, the books of our lives are written by God. Jeremiah 1:5 states, *"before I formed you in the womb I knew you before you*

were born I set you apart; I appointed you as a prophet to the nations. "
God spoke these words to Jeremiah but they are true about all of
us. These short stories are about having my relationship with God
tested on every level. It is easy to trust when things are easy and
smooth. It is easy to trust when your prayer life is on fire, and
your relationship with Our Heavenly Father is on point, but my
Heavenly Father was demanding a much deeper commitment.

For those who may be reading this and is facing a storm, I
encourage you to invite God into this storm. He guarantees that
you will come out on the other side. God has designed us as such
complex and diverse beings, so the challenges we face and the obsta-
cles we meet are different. I believe that even in these differences,
our Heavenly Father shows His commitment to each of us. We
must recognize that we are built for storms, hurricanes, tornadoes,
earthquakes, tsunamis, and every other kind of ferociousness. God
placed everything on the inside of us to withstand the intensity
and velocity of any storm. Our challenge is that we fail to trust and
obey God with the instructions that we are given. For like me, we
often try to rationalize God with our intellect and eventually reach
a conclusion that God certainly did not mean "that." Whatever the
that of our situation is.

Obedience matters! That statement can be the full paragraph,
but to expand, we must recognize that to please God, we must obey
Him in everything. Obedience to God is not a multiple-choice
question. We do not get to select the instances in which we obey.
Obedience is a requirement. Obedience is the first law of God. If we
practice every other law but fail to obey, we have broken the law, and
to break the law is to sin. We then give the enemy the legal right to
accuse us before the Throne of God. Disobedience to God has consequences, for God will not change His laws to accommodate our
acts of rebellion. In 1 Samuel 13:1, God called King David a man
after His own heart, but King David had to suffer the consequences
for his sin of adultery. Moses had such an unusual relationship with
God that He experienced God in unbelievable ways. Moses missed
entering the Promised Land, found in Numbers 20:12, which was a
consequence for his sin of anger.

I love my sons passionately. They both bring our family much joy. They are on their way to becoming young men as of this writing. Being given the responsibility to teach and mold them has brought me deep joy and great satisfaction. They continue to be two gifts from God that I will always treasure. My husband is a very involved Father. He is a spectacular and amazing gift. My husband's support has been the glue that keeps our family stretching and growing for the Glory of God. God gave me another amazing gift when He uprooted me from corporate America in such an unusual way, and here is how it happened.

Our second pregnancy was a surprise. Danny and I would have waited a few years before deciding on Tyler's sibling, but God had other plans. For the Word of God declares in Isaiah 55:8–9 that God's ways are not our ways, and His thoughts are so much higher than our thoughts. Our outlook is limited, but our Father always know the whole story and sees the full picture. During this second pregnancy, the first few months were extremely challenging. My experience was similar to the story of Rebecca in the bible. Rebecca was pregnant with twins who fought in her womb. God told her that she was carrying two nations. I was only pregnant with one child, but the challenges were so severe that I questioned God. God told me to name my son Jeremiah. I disobeyed God's instructions. After Miles's birth, we decided to name him, Miles Julian. There was a real and ongoing fight for my son's destiny. My disobedience allowed Satan to obtain a legal right to access and manipulate Miles's star, thereby interrupting his destiny. The challenges continued in the delivery room. The doctor had to use forceps to assist during Miles's delivery. There were concerns of low heartbeat and ingestion of the amniotic fluid. Additionally, Miles was an unsettled baby with a severe cradle cap. God protected Miles, and I am grateful.

I did not understand this battle. I never knew about each person having a star that holds the secret to our destiny. The wisemen saw Jesus's star, and they followed the star to the place where Jesus was born. This story is found in Matthew chapter 2. I also did not understand or learn about the importance of our names and how being given the wrong name could circumvent God's plans for our lives. You may be skeptical about what I am writing, but let's look for a moment at the story of Jacob (Genesis 25), his name meant "deceiver and supplanter." For a long time in his story, Jacob was a master deceiver. He deceived his father Isaac, to steal his brother Esau's birthright. He deceived his brother and caused Esau to sell his birthright for food. This tendency to deceive was a bloodline issue because his Uncle Laban also deceived him. Jacob married Leah first and then worked seven more years for Rachel, the love of his life, because his uncle Laban deceived him. This behavior was broken in Jacob's life when God changed his name from Jacob to Israel. Jacob's life was transformed. The Bible clearly shows us examples of people whose names were changed for their characters to be converted and their destinies fulfilled. Abram became Abraham. Saul became Paul. And, because of their name changes, they fulfilled their God-given destinies.

During this period in my life, I continued to seek after God passionately. I was a full-time wife, mother, and employee, but I loved the Lord with my heart then and still. One morning just before I woke, Heavenly Father whispered into my spirit that He was taking me out of corporate America. I was excited about this statement because I was in a job that was eating away at my self-esteem. While I made every effort to be efficient and effective as an employee, I was surrounded by others who did not make it easy for me to succeed in my role. My Heavenly Father instructed me that He wanted me to pray twice a day after I was released from my job. I thought to myself that this was going to be an easy task, not recognizing then the discipline and mindset needed to be that focused in prayer. God's word is always true and forever faithful. Although I missed the mark with the naming of my second son and so many other things along the way, God remains faithful. His word declares what the enemy meant for our destruction, He will turn it around for our good and His glory.

The way that God released me from corporate America was through this challenge. The year was 2006, and Miles, was four and a half and was not speaking. This time was difficult for our family. I bombarded heaven on my son's behalf. Those around me who knew how to pray, I encouraged and challenged them to agree in faith with me on behalf of my son. I persisted in prayer, encouraging others to help me to pray. Weekly, Miles was tested by different specialists, each giving their qualified opinions and recommendations. I never connected this challenge to my disobedience in not calling my son by the name that God told me to call him. I objected to most of the recommendations, and I continued to believe God for complete deliverance. I held on by faith to the fact that God had spoken regarding this son that He had given me. I believed all of the promises of God in His word. Every prophet in the Bible was able to speak; I stood in faith, knowing that Miles would also speak.

Finally, after many trying months, the pediatrician recommended immediate aggressive speech therapy. After exploring our options, my husband and I decided that it was in our family's best interest to take advantage of the Family Medical Leave Act (FMLA), which gives a caretaker up to twelve weeks to take care of a sick family member. This time allowed me to be involved in all aspects of our son's care management. But God is so awesome! We were able to release our nanny, and I became the hands-on mother that I desired to be for both of our sons. God used the child that I stepped out of obedience to bring about another blessing in my life. God used these events to release me from corporate America.

Over time, Miles started to use small words, and in time, his vocabulary developed where he spoke sentences. However, his words and sentences were incomprehensible. We continued with speech therapy beyond the twelve weeks. We decided I would resign from my position as a human resources professional. Once again, with the blessing of my husband, we determined that we were going to stay the course with our son Miles' medical care. The added benefit for me as a mother was that I spent time nurturing and molding our sons. During this time, we made the decision as parents to have both sons attend private schools. Financially we were in a stable position to do so, and we needed the flexibility that such a community would provide to assist Miles in the classroom.

Choosing a private school stemmed from several factors. First, education was crucially important to us. The generations who came before us instilled the benefits of obtaining a quality education. Second, we needed small classrooms for our sons, especially to accommodate Miles' limited use of language. Third, my husband grew up in Boston and lived through the tail end of the busing period in Boston's history. A time when Bostons' public schools were under a court mandate to desegregate. History records that this was one of the most turbulent eras in this citys' history. My husband was inadvertently impacted by the effects of this time, he attended eight different schools from kindergarten through his high school years. Several difficult family situations also contributed to Danny's attendance in schools with poor academic performance. During a violent family interaction, his father shot his mother in her leg, which disrupted Danny's family. His mother, now a single parent, moved to low-income housing in the projects. The academic standards across these communities were subpar, and Danny was repeating school-work grade after grade. His mother tried to find a school where Danny could attain a good education, so, each year my husband was in a new school. This instability left a profound mark in Danny's life. When we had our sons, the decision to give them a private school education was easy.

Miles continued to show improvement in his speech, and he attended school with his older brother from 8:30–5pm each day. I now had the opportunity to obey the instruction from God to pray twice a day. I have to tell you that prayer takes a determined commitment. I was already praying on specific nights of the week from midnight to daybreak, but that was much easier than during the day. During those times of the nights, everyone was already sleeping; but during the day, there were so many distractions. Also, now that family and friends knew that I was home, they thought nothing of eating away at my time. I had to be strategic. I dropped the boys at school and completed other priorities. I turned my cell phone off and would sit at my kitchen table with my bible and writing materials and start studying the Word of God. After studying I went into prayer. The first thing that I had to do was take authority over my mind and invite Holy Spirit to pray in me, with me and, for me. I started at first for one hour, and as this became a habit, it became effortless for me to spend hours in My Heavenly Fathers' presence. I was committed and consistent in this instruction. Prayer became my life, and as I continued in prayer, My Heavenly Father started to teach and reveal His secrets to me.

Prayer takes time. Prayer is a personal and an ongoing commitment. Prayer is one of the most essential ways in which we communicate with Our Heavenly Father. It is impossible to have any type of relationship without communication. A stable relationship is centered on good communication. To enjoy a sweet relationship with our Heavenly Father, we must be able to commune with Him in prayer. It is through prayer that we will birth out the things of God in the earth realm. It is through prayer that we have strong families. It is through prayer that we have ministries that have solid foundations. It is through prayer that we counteract the plans and tricks of our enemies. Prayer is an action that we all need to practice. We are all called to pray. I encourage you to stand in your positions and effectively and fervently pray that God's will be done in our lives, homes, communities, nations as it is in heaven.

As Miles grew, his speech impediment became less noticeable, and he was thriving in his early years at school. But you cannot be an intercessor and or a prayer warrior and avoid trouble. The enemy will bring the fight to your very doorsteps. My friends, I am no different. When you desire to live for God, and you are always praying and fasting you are now on hell's radar screen. But I am happy to report that no power can overthrow the power of God. Some events happened in 2010 that are significant. Our sons private school remained affordable and within reasonable distance from our home, but it only went up to the sixth grade. Somewhere around the fifth grade, it became evident that my oldest son, Tyler, needed a change. He needed a more challenging environment, and instinctively, I knew that I had a brief window to find a nurturing environment to continue to capitalize on his learning experiences. I did not know what to do because, every other private school was extremely expensive and much farther away. I did what I had become accustomed to doing—I got on my face (I pray laying face down), and I bombarded heaven regarding this concern.

In February 2010, I was invited to be a guest speaker at a conference in St. Maarten. The call was a surprise, and I was excited and overwhelmed at the same time. I sought God to get his opinion on this matter. Like David, I asked Him, what do you want me to do? God assured me that He wanted me to go and confirmed He would go with me. Indeed, God did just that. He showed up magnificently each night and performed signs, wonders, and miracles. I saw God in the lives that were touched. I saw God returning hope to the hopeless. I saw God showing love and allowing his children to recommit their lives to him.

Upon my return, I received a call from a friend I hadn't spoken to in over two years. She informed me that she was given my phone number in her dream. She stated that she did not know why she needed to speak with me, but she felt an urgency to call. I was surprised, but we fellowshipped on the phone as if we had just spoken the day before. We shared some sweet memories and chuckled at some experiences that we had together. In ending our conversation, I asked her about her daughter. Her daughter was about to graduate from a private school in one of the most prestigious communities in our state. I mentioned to her that I was looking for schools for my sons. She encouraged me to apply and even suggested that she would be willing to make an introduction.

I thought of the impossibilities of maintaining tuitions for two boys, from the fourth and sixth grade through high school. How could I make such a commitment, not knowing how I would follow through to high school? I gave myself every reason why this could not be why she needed to contact me and why pursuing this avenue made no sense for us financially. The average and median household income in this town are some of the highest across the state. I was overwhelmed at the gravity of the challenge. I continued to look at my limitedness and not at God's limitlessness. I continued to see the roadblocks ahead of me, but then my faith rose, and I decided that I would trust God. As I pondered how she remembered my number and the timing of the call, I recognized within myself that this was a God thing. It was just foolish enough to my understanding to be the miracle that I had been asking for.

After I informed my husband of the conversation, I then told him that I would move forward with the application process. And he said to me, *"If that is what God is pushing you to do, do it."* In March 2010, months after many schools had closed their admission process, I submitted applications to the school for my two sons. I have to be honest and tell you I also applied to several other schools. Just in case! How many times do we think that we need a *"just in case, God does not come through plan?"* We were invited to the school for an interview and a walk-through. Upon walking through the school, my oldest son, Tyler, said to us that this is where he needed to be. On our way home, fear took hold of me, and I remember Father saying to me, *"Will you trust me?"* and as I said yes, I felt His peace.

In April 2010, on a family road trip to Canada, The school called, stating that our sons were accepted. We were excited. It was simply amazing to see how God worked this out! Not knowing what would happen in the years ahead, we trusted God believing that he would make a way where there seemed none. Additionally, upon receiving the school's financial aid package, we would be paying close to the same amount in the new school that we were paying at the old school. This was absolutely astounding! God worked on our behalf.

In this new school, Miles adjusted well. There were some challenges, but with help, he overcame them. Miles continued to be a sweet and sensitive child, and one would never be able to tell that he experienced setbacks in his early years. I was just about to get comfortable when he entered middle school, and all hell broke loose. Miles was struggling; he had difficulty in almost every subject. We got him tutors. I was at my wit's end, but because I was in the university of the Holy Spirit, I continued to bombard heaven about this new attack against Miles. I was praying then that my children would be on the honor roll. I was declaring and decreeing it and then it seemed as if the exact opposite was happening. Then toward the end of sixth grade, I met with Miles' teachers, who strongly suggested having Miles tested for a learning disability. Initially, I refused, but a trusted teacher advised me to go through the process to alleviate any doubt.

I never stopped praying; now, I added fasting. One day, the Holy Spirit gave me a strategy. I printed out a picture of a brain. Using that picture, I cried out to God about each part of Miles' brain asking God to bring healing and wholeness. I stood in my place of prayer and holding fast to God's word, I sought His divine intervention. I never wavered. I took Miles for the testing. The results showed that Miles did not have a learning disability. However, the district representative told me if Miles continued to display behaviors in the classroom, he would need to be further evaluated by his pediatrician, who would prescribe medication if needed.

I did not follow through with a visit to the pediatrician. We provided Miles with tutors when necessary, and I continued to provoke God to act on our behalf. Miles continued to struggle throughout his middle school years into high school, and I continued to pray. One of the things that brought some challenges was the level of forgetfulness that Miles experienced. Miles forgot important information. He forgot to study for tests. He forgot homework. He forgot his gym clothes. These episodes of forgetfulness had severe consequences, for we had to travel about one hour and thirty minutes each day, each way to school. So, when he forgot something at home, it cost time in traveling back and forth.

I dreaded the ninth grade, but Miles had to go through it. Miles was trying, but it was evident that his self-esteem was taking a pounding. It was difficult having to struggle with grades, but Miles was also a minority in a predominately white school. I continued to pray and fast. He was not doing well in most of his classes, and math was the worst. Miles failed in math. We were informed that Miles' financial aid for the following school year was in jeopardy. We decided to pull him out of the math class in the middle of the school year. His teachers suggested that Miles be placed on an educational plan that would help him manage his time and classes effectively. He was provided with more tutors. A big piece of this plan required that Miles checked in with his teachers daily. It was one moment during this time that Miles came home, and in speaking with him, I knew that this situation was stealing his confidence and self-esteem. At that moment, I knew that I had to put a stop to all the check-ins that Miles was required to do. I called a meeting informing everyone effective immediately, Miles will no longer check-in with teachers during the school day. Instead, he was going to finish out the school year as quietly as possible. I intended to sign him up at the local public school for summer school for math. Miles breathed a sigh of relief, and although his grades were unsatisfactory, our family settled down to finish the end of the school year.

Throughout these difficult times with Miles, God used a few people to remind me of His promises over Miles's life. Moments when I became despondent in my faith, my Heavenly Father would use one of the handful of people He connected me to, remind me of His faithfulness. The summer of 2018 was a pivotal turning point for Miles and our family. Over the years in the presence of God, He taught me many things, and He also gave me the understanding of names and the importance of names in the spiritual realm. In my heart, I knew that I needed to change Miles's name to Jeremiah, but because of the financial blows that we were experiencing, we never seemed to have any extra money to make the change. One day, one of my sister-friend called and told me she was changing her name. She and her mother shared the same name, and she kept on repeating the same patterns and having similar challenges as her mother. She has had setbacks, delays, hindrances, and she stated that it was time to make a change. My sister-friend said that her name was the culprit. During our conversation, a light bulb went off for me. This step was what I needed to commit to doing for Miles to have the transformation that I was praying for.

After our conversation, I went into prayer, and I asked God's forgiveness for being disobedient to His instruction for not naming Miles, Jeremiah. I had asked for forgiveness before for this very thing, but I took no action to correct the situation. I often told my family that Miles's middle name was Jeremiah, and at times even called him Jeremiah; but I did nothing legally. This time was different because I was desperate! I shared with the family what I intended to do, and I got their blessings. I made a bold declaration that from the moment of Miles's name change that everything, those things that were delayed, denied, stolen, aborted, miscarried—that there would be an immediate repayment and turn around in his life.

In the meantime, Miles started summer school, and I also secured a tutor to assist him during the summer months. I initiated the process for a name change from Miles Julian to Miles Jeremiah. The process for the name change took about a month, and once approved, I legally changed all his records to show his new name as Miles Jeremiah. Things immediately started to change in Miles's life. Suddenly, his confidence that the enemy of our soul stole, started to shine through. In the math class he failed during the school year, Miles received an A in summer school. Working with his tutor, Miles started to grasp mathematical concepts, and what was once difficult started to become somewhat easier. Upon the completion of summer school 2018, Miles walked away with a final grade of A.

Miles went into the new school year, the tenth grade, with renewed courage and confidence that surprised us. To be at school on time, Miles had to leave the house at 6:15 a.m. His brother Tyler worried that Miles was not going to be able to get it together. The Miles that went into the tenth grade was made new by God. Miles's tenth grade year was his best so far. He challenged himself with mentally rigorous subjects, and to the surprise of his teachers, made the honor roll for the first half of the school year. And just in case you may be thinking that God does not hear and answer prayers, Miles made the honor roll again for the second half of the school year. An additional blessing was the full scholarship that Miles received to travel to China with some of his peers for the summer of 2019 on a cultural exchange program. Miles Jeremiah received another scholarship towards his tuition for improvement in all academic areas. These blessings are examples of God's divine repayment.

I will end this chapter by challenging you to get into the deep with God. Invite Him in every aspect of your life and watch Him turn your water into wine (John 2:1–25). I challenge you to obey Him in all things and watch Him give you beauty for ashes (Isaiah 61:13). Samuel told Saul that obedience is better than sacrifice (1 Samuel 15:22). Saul thought that the offering up of the best of the enemy animals was pleasing God, but all God required from Saul was to obey the instructions that he was given. So many times, we offer up sacrifices to God when what He really desires from us is our complete obedience to His will. Let us above all things strive to obey God in all things no matter what the cost.

CHAPTER 4

MY PRAYER DURING DIFFICULT SITUATIONS

"Even though I walk through the darkest valley, I will fear no evil, for you are with me; your rod and your staff, they comfort me. You prepare a table before me in the presence of my enemies. You anoint my head with oil; my cup overflows. Surely your goodness and love will follow me all the days of my life, and I will dwell in the house of the Lord. Forever. Amen." (Psalms 23:4–6)

Father, You are my Rock, my Portion, and my soul trusts in You. I come to You today to remind myself of who I am in you. I stand upon your word and I release them over my life and my situations. I declare that I will fear no evil. I speak to every strong wind and wave, and I command them to be still. Father, You said to Peter, when he came walking to you on the water in the story written in Mathew 14:29, *"Why did you doubt?"* I ask you to strengthen my faith. Let me see my difficult situations through the eyes of faith. Even when I do not understand what You are doing and why You allow these situations to happen, teach me to trust the plans that You have for my life.

Father, help me in this season to keep my eyes on You. I feel the effects of the winds and the waves. I am weary and tired. My feet feel as if they are about to slip. But I release your word that declares in Psalms 121:3, *"He will not let your foot slip. He who watches over you will not slumber."* Today where I need to learn humility, I am ready and willing to learn. Where I need to learn patience, I ask You Father, in the name of Jesus to teach me. I know that You understand my impatient nature. I want things in my time and in my ways. I have a difficult time waiting on you. But teach me to wait for you, My God. You know what is best for me and You are always on time. Even when it is difficult, You, my Father, know the correct temperature and pressure to apply. Thank you for your grace and patience with me. I submit and I give You Lordship in and over my life. I trust You with my life knowing You love me more than I love myself. Thank you for the process in Jesus Name. Amen.

HARD TIMES

Pain alerts the body that something is out of sync. I am often guilty of reacting to the emotion and not address the root cause of the pain. For example, when we have a headache, our first reaction is to grab a tylenol because we desire the ache to go away, but rarely think of the root cause of the pain. This chapter will share some of the deepest pain that we endured. Pain brings out our true character. Looking back in self-reflection to some of the root causes, I recognize that as a family we operated in a spirit of self-sufficiency and pride for many years. Of course, I know that God provides, but the greatest testimony is not when you know how the provision will happen, but when you have not one single clue and you have to trust God to make a way out of no way. The following experiences taught my family that God is consistently reliable even when our situations are speaking louder than Gods' promises.

Our family continued to move forward. Our two sons were in private school, my husband, the sole breadwinner had a full-time stable position. I continued to seek the Lord with all of my heart. Often, we receive a word from the Lord, and we do not understand before we can obtain the fulfillment of the word, we must be processed.

To be processed by God means that God, in His wisdom, introduces circumstances and challenges to prune and prepare us to walk in His purpose for our lives. God knows us individually and designed us uniquely. God uses different methods to crush us. God may process some through a significant crisis, others through trials, difficulties, physical problems, and demanding circumstances. God uses every calamity to bring us to a place of complete dependency on Him, in the course of birthing His purpose in our lives.

Sometimes, the process comes through pain. Our family had some financial stability and were living comfortably. We enjoyed traveling. The thrill of exploring new places brought us joy. During this time, we were able to travel. Life was uninterrupted. Around June 2012, and after some real challenges on his job, my husband, Danny, and his employer made a mutual decision to part ways. Danny did not yet have another employment opportunity. His work situation was depressing. While I knew most of the specifics, to give clarity and peace of mind to the boys, Danny explained his work situation in a family meeting. Danny assured us that we should not be anxious, as he would secure new employment easily and quickly. As his wife, I wholeheartedly supported Danny in his decision. Little did we know that these would be some of the most challenging times in our lives, individually and as a family. But God knows what He is doing and never makes a mistake!

For the remainder of 2012, life continued as usual. My husband took the summer off, and we had some great times and made wonderful memories together as a family. During this time, we had income and health benefits. Danny also applied and received unemployment benefits. The unemployment benefits came with many challenges, for there were long periods when the checks were delayed. We adjusted our spending habits, but there was no real urgency. For the most part, life remained uninterrupted. My husband was casually looking for a job, and while he was not able to secure immediate employment, we still were not very nervous. Then in November of that year, a bomb fell! My mother-in-law informed us that her doctor had diagnosed her with cancer. My first reaction was fear. I did not remember the Word of God that tells us to fear not. My initial reaction was anxiety and fear. After praying, I experienced God's peace and, I reminded myself that God was in complete control.

When 2012 came to an end, our family breathed a sigh of relief. We were stretched in ways that tested our faith. The promises of God for our lives seemed to be on hold, but we continued to experience miraculous answers to our prayers in supernatural ways. Our family were excited to start 2013, it was a new year, and we thought we had been through the fire. We remained confident that God had a plan. As humans, we are limited, it is difficult to trust when we do not understand. We behave like small children, always demanding an explanation to help us understand the reasoning behind the experiences and challenges that we endure. But God is always truthful, always perfect, and though He is an on-time God, He also operates outside of time. We drew from the things that we had passed through in 2012, looking with great expectation toward 2013. We waited in anticipation for the many bold promises that God had spoken over our lives. Little did we know that His plans would carry us way out into the deep, a place that we had never been before.

How is it possible to walk in victory when surrounded by defeat and despair? My husband Danny had not secured employment. Financially, we were approaching a danger zone. The previous employment package had ended along with our health insurance. We had dipped into our savings, so with the little bit that we had left, our only income source was the unemployment check and a three-family rental home where we received rental income every month. The rental amount that we received was only enough to cover that mortgage. Daily we moved forward, trusting in God to meet and supply our needs.

Tuition

There came a time when we could not pay our children's tuition. My first reaction was one of embarrassment. Never having been in this type of situation where I was unable to pay the tuition bill was humiliating. Additionally, my family was one of a handful of minority families, and I did not want to be characterized as a cliché. The boys continued to attend school, and I continued to volunteer within the school community. It took great courage for me to continue to be a part of the community. The spirit of shame was speaking louder than the promises of God. I kept focused and remained faithful in prayer. There came a time when my husband suggested that I started to look for another school for the boys. My response was that God did not tell me to move them. My faith was crazy enough to see how God was going to bring us through this challenge. I am grateful to God for His favor. I understand His favor more today than back then. God's favor is evidence that a person has God's approval. Gods' favor is evident when others, even your enemies, go out of their way to do that thing that they said that they would never do for you. In retrospect, God's favor was all over my family then and still is today.

I cannot tell you the number of times my husband and I met with the school's business office. These meetings started in 2013 and continued through 2018. I continued to follow the Lord's instruction to pray, and not only did I pray during the day, but I started the habit of getting up at 2:00 a.m. to seek the face of the Lord. Each time a meeting was called, I was on my face in prayer at 2:00 in the morning asking God for His intervention. What I really wanted God to do was to bless me in such a way that I would never have to worry about having the ability to pay anything again. I was tired of feeling humiliated. Everything that God allows in our lives has a purpose, even our pain has purpose. If you are reading this book and are looking at a challenge that seems humiliating, remember that God will bring purpose from your pain. Keep trusting God. He knows what He is doing, and He will never disappoint you. It was important for me to stay strong, as not to discourage my husband, who still had not secured employment. We continued to pray and trust God.

We saw the hands of God moving in different ways, but two incidents stand out that I need to share with you. During the summer of 2014, I received a call from the business office one week before our sons returned to school. The caller informed me that our sons' tuition was long overdue, and if their tuition were not paid in full, my youngest son, Miles Jeremiah (his amount was greater) would not be allowed to return to school. He would not even be allowed on the school grounds. My husband was at home when I received the phone call, but I did not share the conversation with him. I stopped what I was doing and went into my son's room. I got down on my face before God, my Employer. I cried out to God, telling Him that this was a moment of deep embarrassment. I poured out my heart to Him, asking for His help. Then I remember saying, but like the three Hebrew boys, their story found in Daniel 3, I still will not bow. Shadrach, Meshach, and Abednego were three Hebrew boys in captivity in Babylon. They were given Babylonian names; their Babylonians handlers tried to get them to eat the king's food, which was offered up to Babylonian gods. Additionally, the king wanted them to worship a golden image. They refused. As a result, these three boys were thrown into a fiery furnace made seven times hotter. In the end, God showed up in the furnace and delivered them. I told God that even in the fire, I would trust Him. I was still in the moment of crying and praying when the phone rang again. Recognizing that it was the school again, I jumped and answered. It was the same lady on the other end. She informed me that she had made a mistake and was calling to tell me that she was extremely sorry. She informed me both of my boys would be able to attend the school, which started the following week.

The Head of School is a dedicated and compassionate leader. She loves every student, and this is evident in her commitment to them. Danny and I met with her and members of her team. When my husband and I walked in, I was nervous, embarrassed, and anxious. I did not know what to expect. Yes, I had prayed, but I thought this was the meeting where the school informed us that we had to leave. I was trying to keep my faith, but felt pressed on every side. The constant demands for meetings were wearing on us, and being in this type of fire was uncomfortable. The meeting convened, and again, like countless times before, we shared the status of where we were financially. The message was the same, Danny had not secured employment, and we were unable to meet our financial responsibilities to the school.

Eventually, the Head of school stated there was a waiting list of families who were eager to get into the school. She said that she had spoken to the Board and informed them that the school needed our family there. She then spoke about our family in glowing terms and advised the business office that they should make a financial arrangement with us that makes the best sense for our family and the school. That was God, showing His kindness and favor to our family once again. As I write this story, Tyler has graduated from this school and is attending college. Miles Jeremiah is in his senior year. We are still challenged financially with tuition, but God is God over the big and small things. To God be the glory!

Mortgages

I would not blame our financial challenges only on lack of employment, everything that happened was a plan from the enemy to circumvent God's promises in our lives. The enemy's assignment is to kill, steal, and destroy. This is what the enemy wanted to do in our family, and with families everywhere. But the Word of God says in Romans 8:28, *"All things work together for the good of those who love the Lord."* This Word remains true. If you are going through difficult situations right now as a child of God, even though you may not see how this would bless you eventually, know that it is working for your good. God still turns oceans into highways and water into wine.

Our backs were against the wall. Financially everything was falling apart. It was going on months, and after several interviews, Danny could not secure employment. I also started to look for employment opportunities, and absolutely no doors were opened. I persisted in prayer with fasting. The entire family went on a thirty-day fast. The boys fasted from fast food. Danny and I went nineteen days without food and the remaining days, had meals after 4:00 p.m. The enemy was hunting, and we needed God to fight for us. Our extended family knew that Danny was not working, but we did not ask for help from anyone, neither did we share with anyone what we were going through. The not asking and not sharing was not because of pride it was merely the place that God had positioned us for that season. The Word of God said that Jesus had to go through Samaria to meet the woman at the well (John 4:4–42) this story talks about Jesus going into Samaria specifically to meet an adulterous woman. What Jesus did was meet her to change her story. As a family, we had to go through this time of testing so that God could transform us. He needed to transform how we trust Him, and our relationship with Him, so we had to go through this season of testing.

Six months in this dry place and our mortgages, which were always promptly paid, were way behind. At that time, we had our home and a rental property. Things were so bad that the money that was being paid for the rent was what we were using to live. Our bills were behind, and our dry place started to resemble a barren desert. I stayed the course in prayer, and since my husband was home during these times, he also joined me in prayer. Before this point, my husband knew of God through my devotion to God. We had gotten to a place where I could now pray openly in our home. He knew that I spent time in prayer and studying the Word of God, but he had no idea the level of commitment and focus. During those two years at home, this intense focus of prayer, study, and fasting helped us through the process and brought Danny into a strong relationship with God.

I prayed for God's intervention, but what I needed more than anything else was His strength. There were moments of weakness, but I could not afford to show my family that weakness and uncertainty in my faith. I needed to encourage them even when I needed encouragement. I ran into God's presence, for I was desperate. In His arms were the only place that I felt safe. I did not like being stretched in this way. It was painful and uncomfortable. The battle was fierce, hard, and long. My family and I were becoming tired, and I often wondered during those times what did I do wrong. It is in those moments of weakness where doubt and unbelief start clouding our minds. There were days that I repeated scripture after scripture because the voices of doubt and unbelief were always screaming at me.

I built up enough courage to contact the mortgage company for our primary residence. Our monthly mortgage amount was roughly $2,200. At this point, we were about three months behind. In our years of owning our home, this was the first time that we had ever been overdue in our monthly payment. Our credit up to that time was exemplary. I did not know what to expect, and I was afraid of what I would hear. On the phone, I met one of the most kind and understanding mortgage representatives. I shared our story, and she immediately sent the required paperwork for us to complete. She

informed me that the mortgage company would review the paperwork and respond with an amount that would be feasible for us. I
breathed a sigh of relief and waited to hear what the response would
be. About one week later, we heard from the mortgage representative,
the conversation went like this:

Mortgage rep: "Hello, Mrs. Best, we have reviewed the paperwork
and wanted to know if you can afford 25."
My Response: "Twenty-five hundred?" in an incredulous voice.
Mortgage Rep: "No! I meant $25 a month for the next six months."

I was shocked. I did not know how to react. We were given a
grace period of six months to pay that amount. The mortgage company advised us to communicate with them if our employment situation changed. That was all God! I was grateful for His goodness and
grace shown to us.

We still had other pressing financial concerns. We needed to
pay tuition and the mortgage payments on the rental property. I persisted in prayer with fasting. I submitted my petitions to God. I had
no other recourse. Eventually, we received notice that the lender on
our rental property was going to initiate foreclosure proceedings if
we did not bring the loan up to date. This would be a big embarrassment. How could I testify that I am serving the Living God and
be brought to shame in this way? As is my custom, I went before
the Lord around 2:00 a.m. and submitted my complaints to Him. I
reminded Him of His Word in Isaiah 49:23, *(AMP) "I am the Lord;
for they shall not be put to shame who wait for, look for, hope for, and
expect Me. Isaiah 49:23b (CWR) I am the Lord and that those who
put their hope in me and wait for my help will not be disappointed."*
I praised and worshipped Him and finally went back to bed. Upon
returning to bed, I dreamt that I saw my mother-in-law giving me a
big bag of money.

I shared the dream with my husband. We prayed and waited
to see what the Lord was going to do. Two days later, I received a
call from my mother-in-law stating that she needed to speak to me.
As I sat down to listen, she started by saying that she knew that

Danny was not working, and she had been troubled in her spirit. What a Wonderful Savior! After several conversations with Danny and myself, God moved on her heart to bless in a significant way, which enabled us to cancel out the pending mortgage procedures and help with tuition for the boys' school. God is so wise in all that He does, and even though we do not see and sometimes do not understand, God really desires us, his children, to totally depend and trust in Him.

Interviews

Danny is a wonderful husband and father who has come to know and love the Lord. Our family were experiencing severe challenges, but as painful as these times were, they brought us closer to God and each other. When God desires our attention, He will use whatever He pleases. God had our full attention! If you are reading this book, and all hell has broken loose in your life, I challenge you to try Jesus. Jesus loves you! He is a present help in the times of trouble, and if it is one thing that we can be sure of in this life is that trouble will come. John 16:33 *"I have told you these things, so that in me you may have peace. In this world you will have trouble. But take heart! I have overcome the world."* We never have to face challenges by ourselves, and because our Father has overcome the world, then we too can overcome.

For almost two years, Danny was unable to secure a position. This was difficult for us as a family. As a man who prides himself as a provider for his family, every interview broke him a little inside. Danny had over eighty interviews over two years. As his wife, it was stressful to see my husband hurting, but I knew that God needed to crush us so that His glory would be seen in our lives. In one situation, Danny went to three separate interviews and met with over eight different individuals. The company started to check his references, and we were hopeful this was an employment opportunity. That Saturday morning, God woke me up early and had me intercede on Danny's behalf. By the time Danny woke up, he received word that he was not selected for the role. Danny was devastated, and I was disappointed.

There was no consolation. We held onto each other, cried, and prayed for God's will to be done. Sometimes God's will and our desires are out of sync. God will orchestrate situations to reconcile our will to His. What we endured taught us how to surrender our will to the plan and purpose of God. The beauty of this season was the times that we laid on the floor together, seeking the face of God. The times we spent studying the Word of God. Times when we no longer knew what to pray, so we danced to gospel music. The times when Danny would immerse himself in baking and preparing family dinners. It may have been the worst of times, but it also was the best of times. We were pressed on every side, but our home was full of the presence of God. We enjoyed God's joy and His peace, and for that, we were grateful. The story of the three Hebrew boys, Shadrach, Meshach, and Abednego, strongly resonated with Danny because they came out of the furnace of fire, their hair unsinged, and clothes not burnt, and they did not smell like smoke. I want to remind you that you will not smell like the fire you are going through and coming out of in Jesus Name.

Finally, God prepared a table for Danny in the presence of our enemies. Danny was going back into the workforce a little bruised and broken but with memorable experiences and testimonies about the acts of God. Danny had a more profound love and relationship with our Heavenly Father.

How many of us have been in a place of total dependency on God? These places are sometimes extremely uncomfortable and could bring feelings of hopelessness and anxiety. But I hear the Word of the Lord saying in Philippians 4:6, *"Be anxious for nothing, but in everything by prayer and supplication with thanksgiving let your requests be made known to God."* It is often difficult to trust. Trust means a total reliance on the integrity, strength, the ability of a person. Learning to trust God means that we must have experiences that teach us that He is trustworthy.

There are so many other experiences that I have not included in this chapter. The instances that we drove the boys to and from school on an empty tank. The times that we had to sell soda cans to put gas in the car. The times that we had to secure health insurance through the state and the experiences that we endured. The impact on our credit. I could continue but God is faithful. Yet we never went without food. We did not apply for food stamps (there is nothing wrong with using food stamps). The decision was an unconscious one because we always believed that things were going to be better. The thanksgiving season of 2014 met us with no money and not enough food for a meal—the day before, we received one hundred dollars. We were able to purchase food for our dinner. God always provided. God kept us in good health. Today I can say that these experiences are still working for the good of my family.

Car Troubles

For faith to grow and become strong, it will be tested by the fiery circumstances of our lives. Our family navigated the turbulence of our situations, but we were exhausted from our troubles. One profound memory from that time was picking up my son, Miles, from school, and upon entering the car, he was excited to see that the tank was full of gas. We were weary. My faith wavered and was weak and small at times. I took comfort from Ecclesiastes 9:11 that encourages us that the race is not for the swift, nor the battle to the strong, but the race is for those who endure to the end.

Trouble bombarded us on every side. We held on with our small faith and watched as God answered our prayers. Our faith grew. We started to walk with assured confidence in God. We did not know when, but we knew that better days were ahead. Surely our situation could not get any worse; then it did.

We lived in a city, but our home is a distance from public transportation. Our sons traveled one and one-half hours each day, each way to get to and from school. We had two old reliable cars. However, when the enemy is allowed to touch us, he will leave no stone unturned. Satan's assignment is to kill, steal, and destroy. Our cars were not exempt from his onslaught. My husband's car started to stall on the road. This new onslaught caused a level of anxiety, for we travel on several different highways each day. To have our car stalling on the road was not only humiliating but dangerous. We took the car to several mechanics. Every quote to fix the car was unaffordable. Finally, we connected with a mechanic who was a friend of the family. After he examined our car, he told us that it was not worth repairing. He advised us to invest the money in a new car. What a joke! We were out of options. We had no money. Our credit was shattered, and we were overwhelmed.

It looked hopeless, but we decided to take the car to the dealer with faith that God would give us His favor. The dealer gave us one hundred dollars for our battered vehicle. With our low credit scores and a small amount of money down, we secured a newer car. We were happy with our new, more dependable vehicle, however with severely damaged credit and no significant down payment, we entered a financially brutal deal with an extremely high-interest rate that mostly benefited the lender. In spite of this, we were grateful.

God can and God will. God allows all situations for a purpose. Many times we do not see the reason until after we have walked through the challenges. If you are dealing with insurmountable challenges, remember that God can. He is not holding out on you, and He has not forgotten you. He is not absent and uncaring. He is present. He is intentional in what He allows in our lives. Where you are weak, allow God to strengthen you. Cast every problem on Him because He truly cares about you. Be reminded, as God reminded King Hezekiah in 2 Chronicles 20:15, *"this battle is not yours, but it belongs to the Lord."*

CHAPTER 5

MY SISTER-FRIEND PRAYER

Father, O how I adore you! Today I exalt your name for your name is great and greatly to be praised. Amen. Today I come, and I surrender and submit to your will. I desire to bring you glory and praise and honor. I ask your forgiveness of my sins. I am grateful to you for every gift you have given me, sometimes these gifts are in the form of relationships that you have divinely orchestrated and I am so ever thankful.

Father, I thank you for my sister-friends. You are so wise, and I love your wisdom. You have placed around me women who love you and desires to please you in every area of their lives. You have connected us in such an unusual way and have given us the capacity to see each other through the eyes of love. Your Word declares that love is kind and patient. Father, teach us to exercise kindness and patience with each other. Let us not be boastful, proud, or envious of one another. Father, in the Name of Jesus, we live in a time where it is said that women are petty, catty, and materialistic. We reject those words from our lives and declare that we are of a different caliber of women. We carry the DNA of our Heavenly Father, and that makes us different. Our words are seasoned with your wisdom, so when we speak, the wisdom of God is heard. Our presence is filled with your peace, so wherever we go your peace mantles the atmosphere surrounding us.

I thank you that we are wise master builders. Your Word says in Proverbs 14:1, *"A wise woman builds her home, but a foolish woman tears it down with her own hands."* Father, in the Name of Jesus, we build our husbands, children and relationships in wisdom. We will not allow our attitudes, words, and actions destroy what you are calling us to build. Grant us the ability to understand. Let us be slow to anger and eager to listen. Father, you know as women that we are emotional by nature; this is how you have designed us. But today, I ask in the Name of Jesus that you heal us in our emotions. Some of us are carrying deep emotional secret scars. We do not want anyone to know our shameful experiences. Teach us your truth and teach us to desire truth in every area of our lives. Father, You have pulled us from different cultural backgrounds and brought us together as sister-friends. None is more important than the other. Teach us to be humble, and give us hearts that can accept correction, in Jesus name. I thank you for my sister-friends and for the experiences that you allowed us to have individually and collectively. Let your will be done in our lives, homes, and families today and forevermore in Jesus name I ask these things, in Jesus name I thank you. Amen.

THE GIRLFRIEND FACTOR

Hard times is described as passing through severely, difficult circumstances. I cannot express, in words, the palpable relief that I felt when 2013 closed. I had never endured such uncertainty, and I had never been spiritually stretched in my faith. 2013 was one year that I would never want to relive. I believed our family had endured the worst of our challenging circumstances. I was wrong! The pressing had just begun, and 2013 was the prelude for more to come. Throughout 2013, God did not allow me to walk alone. God is so faithful that even when we are in pressing situations, He sends help.

God is wise! My circle of girlfriends, who I refer to as sister-friends was always very small. During these times, it was the four of us going through our different circumstances. My sister-friends knew each other through their relationships with me. We were at different stages in our life and in our relationship with Christ, but we forged a stronger sister-ship through the challenges we experienced. My sister-friends are fiercely loyal. First to God and then to our sistership. I am not sure which of us was more relieved to see 2013 end, for each of us walked out of 2013 battle weary. Our faith was pushed to the brink, and we had wounds that only God, and time, would heal. In this friendship of four, three of us were married and one divorced. The strangeness about our situation was that we were in three different states, disconnected by distance but connected by God. We know that God is everywhere, and His presence supersedes time, distance, and space. Mention the year 2013 to any of us and we may have similar reactions. Cold sweat mixed with anxiety! We had some experiences that we do not want to revisit. Sit with anyone of us and we can show you the scars that we received from the battles that we went through. Yet, each of us can testify of the Majestic Power of the Almighty God that we serve. He is able to keep, and to satisfy.

We stood side by side and back to back in prayer. It was as if we were in the birthing chamber being a midwife to each other. Giving birth is a painful and messy process. The pain, the different noises, the smells becomes overwhelming. One moment, you want to push, the next moment you want something to drink, then in the next moment you want to scream. Every emotion and desire rise to the top at the same time. It is critical when giving birth that the midwives are experienced, skilled, and flexible, being able to balance the different aspects of what is going on in the birthing room. The delivery is a fast-paced environment, preparing for the receiving of the baby.

The delivery room is a place of deep intimacy, and one is often selective of who you invite in this place. The wisdom of God in our sister-friendship is that while our challenges were different, we had situations that bound us together. We were midwives to each other, we were too desperate to be ashamed. We needed God's intervention and direction more than judgment and condemnation. We encouraged, we cried, we prayed with each other. God orchestrated the seasons of our lives, that together, we confronted our challenging circumstances. We were midwives to each other as we comforted, confronted, reassured, and strengthened one another.

Scripture tells us of such relationships between women. Naomi and Ruth's story found in the Book of Ruth had an extraordinary bond. Naomi and Ruth's deep pain interrupted their comfort zone. These two women were faced with severe loss and needed direction. Naomi thought that this was end for her, she was willing and ready to return to her people with a shameful and hopeless heart. Ruth, her daughter-in-law, so honored Naomi that she willingly decided to return to Naomi's country with her. This decision placed them in a precarious situation. Widows in the bible days were without protection. Widows did not have anyone to provide for them, so they were often exploited and abused. Naomi and Ruth were widows, homeless, poor, and vulnerable. They did not understand that God was behind the scenes of their lives to bring about a greater purpose. When God is ready for His Divine purposes to be fulfilled, He will shake us out of those patterns, habits, and comfort zones that are necessary for us to be what He has called us to be. God will place trusted, godly women in our lives to midwife us to the next level. We know how the story of Ruth and Naomi ended, and we know that it is through this bloodline that Jesus the Savior of the world made His appearance.

Elizabeth and Mary in the Gospel of Luke also shared an unusual relationship. Both were pregnant through a miraculous act of God. Elizabeth was about eighty years old in her sixth month of pregnancy with John the Baptist, while Mary was pregnant with Jesus when they met. Their stories did not make sense to the natural man. I cannot even imagine Mary trying to explain to her parents and peers that she was a virgin but pregnant with a child. God sometimes does not make sense in the ways He brings about His promises!

Yet Mary's instruction was to visit Elizabeth, who also had an unbelievable miracle. At eighty years of age, (my mother-in-law's age), God remembered Elizabeth and blessed her womb, taking away her shame. For in those times, it was shameful not to have an heir to carry on your name. God redeemed Elizabeth even in her old age. Mary's instruction was to go to Elizabeth because they were both having unusual experiences. They could midwife each other through these miraculous events. They were able to relate to each other. They were able to encourage and support each other. They were able to pray for each other. It was Elizabeth and Mary against the skeptics of their times. There were no jealousy, envy, gossiping, judgment, and condemnation in these relationships. There was only love, acceptance, and empowerment of each other. Each woman fulfilled their purpose in each other's life. These relationships were divinely inspired by God, as was our relationships.

Scars are sometimes invisible. Sometimes they fade, and sometimes they are hidden. Often we walk around with faded, hidden scars with a story that not many do not know. It is important to remember that while scars may be invisible, the memories remain. Every scar has a story. As sister-friends, we limped out of 2013 with scars reminding us of what we came through. I will share some of my sisters story to help you understand some of the battles that we endured.

Death and Despair

Sister-friend number one was the youngest of the group. She has a sweet spirit. She is resilient and focus. Her faith is strong, and her love for the Lord is evident. She recently married and was excited about her first pregnancy, a first baby for both she and her husband. We were all very happy for them. She flooded me with pictures of her growing bump kept me informed of the different stages that she was going through. Life was good. We continued to support her with prayers and encouragement as her delivery date drew closer. Toward the last month of her pregnancy, she like millions of women before her developed swelling. Having had the same situation with my first pregnancy, this was not an alarming red flag.

We continued to pray and remained joyous at the arrival of the baby. We talked about how life-changing this event was going to be, because they were always traveling. It was one day before her due date and we were over the moon. I could not wait to hear what her experiences would be during labor. We laughed about not taking an epidural and going through the process naturally. We chuckled as I explained that I went through the process naturally with an epidural. Danny and I were excited and having a good time. Then we got the most earth-shattering call from her husband. During her regular scheduled appointment, there was no movement in her womb. One day before her due date, the baby died. As a result, on the due date, she had to give birth to a lifeless baby. Words could not truly express the sense of loss and despair that we felt. We were inconsolable! As mothers, we felt her pain, and as friends, we were helpless.

We turned to God who consoled and comforted our sister and her family. Our faith was shaken, but our confidence in God remained firm. This loss was devastating! My sister lived in another state; distance separated us. Our family did not have the resources to go to be with her family. Some days, we held on by a thread, and other days, it was God Himself who carried us. This was not the outcome that we expected. The depth of this pain would only subside by the healing power of God. Today I am happy to report that God has blessed my sister with two healthy, beautiful children. They are a joy and delight to her family and to all who meet them. After one season comes another. God is the architect of the times and seasons of our lives.

Betrayal

My second sister-friend is strong, loyal, and considerate with a heart of kindness. She loves the Lord and constantly recognizes His hand in her life. She was married for many years, and we have enjoyed a wonderful and sweet friendship throughout the different seasons of our lives. Like the experiences of many other women in relationships, we have endured heartaches, losses, and loneliness. Intuitively, we know when things are out of sync in our relationships. We are women, built with an internal alarm.

Betrayal is a violent act and causes a breach of trust. Relationships are complicated, for no two individuals are alike. What makes relationships work is the commonality of the individuals involved, their willingness to compromise, compounded by trust. Trust is an essential ingredient in a relationship. The ability to trust others becomes stronger through proven opportunities that show trustworthiness. Compromise and trust are necessary components to build a harmonious relationship. When trust is destroyed, relationships take time, work, and effort to be completely restored. When trust is violated, we want to move forward without addressing the violation. Restoring trust takes forgiveness, healing, patience, understanding, and love; for the foundation of trust is broken.

My second sister experienced deep betrayal from one that she loved deeply and passionately. This betrayal shook the foundation of the relationship, but it also made her question herself. How do you continue to trust God and have faith when everything you believe is shaken? It is often difficult to move forward after such an act has taken place. There are days we do not know how to pray. Like children, we ask Him why? When we think that God does not respond, we become anxious, wanting the pain and hurt to go away. We do not want to go through the process. Like Naomi and Ruth, we love our comfort zones. We cannot plan for the unknown, so we want to remain in our comfort zones.

God, who loves us richly, allowed Jesus to experience the shame and pain of the cross. He sat and watched as nails pierced Jesus' hand. He watched when they placed a crown of thorns on Jesus head. He watched when they took the scourge and beat Jesus, causing his back to bleed. Yet Our Heavenly Father knew that Jesus had to go through this and gave Jesus the grace that was needed to endure. God knows there are times we must go through the difficult places, but, when we get through our test, our testimony will help others. My second sister held on to God with everything. When her faith was small, I joined my faith to hers and we took small steps forward. There were days if you were following us, you would see the drops of blood trails because we were bleeding. We look back and we thank God for His strength that kept us, His grace that kept our minds and the confidence that He gave us that we are victorious.

Betrayal is painful, and many think that it is sometimes an unforgivable act. We must forgive. God commands us to forgive, as He forgives us. Forgiveness is not a choice; it is a command. I, like many others, have experienced the bitter sting of betrayal. Betrayal hurts. Betrayal is crippling and brings torment. Betrayal makes us question our value and our ability to trust others. Betrayal rocks our self-confidence, and it sometimes changes how we think about ourselves and others. Betrayal keeps us stuck, unable to move forward in life. Betrayal cripples us and prevents us from loving, growing and living life to our fullest potential. Healing is a process; it takes time. God specializes in healing hearts. I encourage you to choose forgiveness. Allow God to heal the hurts and deal with the pain of betrayal you have experienced in your situations.

Disappointment

My third sister is divorced and is the oldest among us four. She has a wealth of wisdom and experiences that I tap into to avoid repeating her mistakes. She is sincere, generous, and straight-forward. My third sister has a rich relationship with God. She loves the Lord and lives a life that reflects that love each day. Her faith carried me many times. My third sister loves what she does for a living, and having a job was/and is vital to her, being a single woman, and needing to provide for herself.

God gave her His assurance that He will keep her employed. After receiving that word and being reassured and comforted by that word everything started to go wrong. The opposite of what God spoke to her started to happen. The hours of her full-time forty-hour position started to become less and less until eventually, she did not have any hours at all. It is important to note that most times, when God gives us a word the enemy of our soul fights to counteract the word given.

My third sister was now at home without employment. She was actively looking for work, but her financial responsibilities started to become difficult. Meeting her financial obligations was challenging. Several months passed, and every door appeared to be closed. Not only closed but bolted from the inside. Nothing was moving, and God seemed to be silent on the matter. What do you do when hell breaks loose against you? How do you stand when your feet become weak? We stood back to back, and prayed. We cried, but we prayed. We fasted and prayed. We shook off hopelessness, and when unbelief and doubt knocked, we kept them at bay with the Word of God. Finally, in the third month, my third sister got a job. This was not her ideal position. but brought some money into her hands. It was a far distance away. She prayed for the right attitude, and each day went into work, still trusting God to honor His Word.

My third sister worked on that job for a short while. During those times, we fasted often. We decided to fast because we needed clarity, and we needed to remain spiritually alert. These challenges open the door for the spirit of disappointment. The spirit of disappointment is so subtle. One would be waiting on a promise from God, and because that promise did not manifest within the time frame we expect, disappointment steps in. If we are not careful, we would not be able to identify it as disappointment. This spirit will convince you that God has deserted you, that God did not say that. This spirit will start affecting the way you see God and the way you see yourself. The spirit of disappointment will impact your life, and eventually, it will steal your joy and kill your hope. That is the assignment of the enemy, to kill, steal, and destroy.

In the fourth month after this vicious attack, God restored my sister's employment. It started with a few shifts a week and not the full-time schedule that she lost. We started to declare God's promises boldly standing in our authority. One of the benefits of fasting and praying is the confident boldness that is received. Although restoration had began, it was but a trickle. We recognize that eight and sixteen hours a week was not full restoration, so instead of praying and crying out to God we started to boldly declare that employees must call out of their shifts making room for my sister. As we declared it to be so, we stood back and watched God bringing the declaration to pass. We did this until she had full restoration with overtime as a bonus. God gave us victory. His word says that none that put their trust in Him shall be put to shame. God is absolutely faithful, and no one can be compared to Him.

The enemy of our soul hates us with a passion, and his plan is to cause us to miscarry and abort the purposes of God for our lives. The enemy's strategy becomes effective when we have an identity crisis and fail to weaponize ourselves according to Ephesians 6:12 *"For we wrestle not against flesh and blood, but against principalities, against powers, against the rulers of the darkness of this world, against spiritual wickedness in high places."* Each piece of our armor is important to protecting ourselves against the constant attack that is formed against us. God gave my sister-friends and me each other in those times when it may have appeared that we were defenseless and powerless. Although we had our individual challenges, we were not weak at the same time. We held on to the faith that we had, and when our faith waivered, we leaned on each other. We invited God in and surrendered to the process.

Completely surrendering to anything for any length of time is extremely difficult, putting others in control often goes against human nature. As sister-friends, we had a choice and we determined to trust God. How do you trust when your heart is hurting? How do you trust when you have been betrayed? Or when you have lost your firstborn child? How do you trust God with no money? The formula that worked for us then, and I know that it will work for you is this; we prayed, fasted, and gave God back His word. In moments when our words became inadequate and repetitive, we quoted God's Word. His Word works! We pushed forward completely trusting that God will work out His plans for our lives.

The beauty of this time was because of our deep desperation, we came before God naked and unashamed. God kept us, and today while we have the scars to remind us of what we have been through, we also have the testimonies that prove that God is our Keeper and our Shade. We were and still are midwives to each other. The friendship of my sisters is a gift that is a blessing from God.

CHAPTER 6

MY PRAYER FOR HEALTH AND HEALING

Father in the name of Jesus, I proclaim You Lord over my life, home, marriage, children, and the businesses You have placed in my hands. This day, I declare that you are my God, my Father, and my King. This day I come to you asking for your mercy, for your forgiveness. I repent of every intentional and unintentional sin.

Today, I present my body as a living sacrifice, holy, acceptable unto God, which is my reasonable service. Father, I thank you for how you have designed my body. I thank you that you took your time and made me wonderfully and fearfully. I thank you that when you looked at the final handiwork that you said that I was good. Teach me to accept and appreciate myself so I may bring honor and glory to your name.

Today, Father, I thank that you say in your word beloved I wish above all things that you prosper and be in good health even as your soul prospers. Today, Father, I come against every plan and scheme of the enemy against our health and healing in Jesus name. Your word declares that healing is your children's bread, and because we are your blood-bought children, we eat the bread of healing today. I speak healing and wholeness over every system in our bodies. I command our bodies to reject any hidden seed that is not from God, in Jesus name. I speak a prophetic word to our very blood that sustains us, and I command our blood to reject sickness and diseases in the Name of Jesus. I ask you today to make us whole. I come to you asking you to break every evil and reoccurring pattern of sickness over my life. Let every evil foundation receive the fire of God. Today let every evil foundation burn from its very root in Jesus name. I ask in Jesus name that you break every evil boundary line of sickness and disease. I thank you that the boundary lines have fallen upon us in pleasant places. We have a beautiful heritage. This is who we are and only because of you, my Father. Today, I give you our hearts, examine our hearts and let every chamber bring you glory in Jesus's Name. Amen.

HEALING IS THE CHILDREN'S BREAD

Our family continued to press forward into the future. There was no doubt that we were at war! We were on the enemy radar screen, and everything and anything was thrown at us. This battle was a war for our destinies. We took hits after hits as trouble came to us in waves after waves. As soon as one event quieted down, another event was not too far on the horizon. At times, the noise from the camp of the enemy caused me to fear. Other times, the voices of doubt and anxiety prevailed over my mind. If God had told me before the fact that for the next five years, rough seas and strong winds were going to take place, I would have prepared. But I had no advanced warning. These rough seas and strong winds were pushing me outside of my comfort zone. I remained committed to prayer and fasting, but the battles were intense!

I took courage from our brother Job who experienced troubles on every level. The words of his complaint found in the book that carries his name Job 23 comforted me. It states in verse 8–10, "*If I go forward, he is not there; or backward; I cannot perceive him; [9] on the left he hides, and I cannot behold him; I turn to the right, but I cannot see him. [10] But he knows the way that I take; when he has tested me, I shall come out like gold.*"

If this was a test, I wanted to pass, but one cannot underestimate the level of mental, emotional, physical, and spiritual grit that is needed to hold onto the promises of God, when all of hell has broken loose against you. Our God is a shelter in the times of storms. God covered and secured my family when we lacked strength and courage. Our bodies are important. We have bodies so that we can legally operate in the earth realm. Nothing and no one can function in the earth realm without a body. God uses us through the indwelling of the Holy Spirit that lives in us. So too, the enemy uses people's bodies to carry out his agenda against the children of God. We must remember that whatever God does, the enemy always counterfeits. Our health is essential. When we have good health, we can enjoy the life that God has gifted and ordained us to live. It is not surprising then that time and time again, we are attacked with sicknesses and diseases, and we forget the word of God declares that healing is the children's bread.

These words found in the story of the Canaanite woman in the book of Matthew chapter 15. The story is profound because this Gentile woman exhibited courage when out of desperation, she sought out Jesus for the healing of her daughter. Jesus responded by saying that healing was for the children He was sent to redeem; but because of her faith and God's grace, her daughter received complete healing. Bread symbolizes food and nourishment. Food is what sustains and keeps our bodies healthy and whole.

The attack against our health started when my mother-in-law, one of my staunchest and dearest friends, informed us that her doctor found a spot on her lungs. Additional tests and x-rays were conducted, and the results came back as cancerous. My mother-in-law told us that there was an immediate need to operate. This diagnosis meant that she would have to have surgery, and according to the doctor's report, the surgery would be followed by months of chemotherapy. The news was devastating, but when I heard it, the peace of God came over me. I reminded myself that no matter the outcome that God had the last word and the final say. God works in mysterious ways, and I must trust him.

My mother-in-law, is referred to as Ma, and I share a deep and close bond. I am married to her youngest son for the past twenty-three years, and we have a lot in common. Before I continue, let me share a brief overview of the relationship between my mother-in-law and myself and how God intervened to show His Glory in our family.

My husband and I were looking to purchase our first home. I prayed and asked God for some specific items. I told My Heavenly Father that I wanted a big house, with a big yard on a cul-de-sac. I did not pray about location. I just prayed in that way and allowed him to lead us. We were four years married then, and we looked for homes for a while but found nothing compelling on the market. With our first son Tyler's arrival to the family, we made the necessary adjustments and resumed our home hunting again. We lived in the city, and both our parents and other family members were about five minutes away from where we lived. It never occurred to us to look outside of those areas. We unconsciously decided that we wanted to remain close to family members. But God is wise and so trustworthy!

Danny eventually suggested that we look outside of the areas that we desired. We drove to the suburbs south of the city to explore further. On our way, we drove past an open house sign and decided to stop. We went into the neighborhood which was newly developed, houses were being built, it was a cul-de-sac that had great potential. The house with the open house sign was big with a huge yard, and Father added a bonus, it was new construction. We immediately fell in love and placed an offer. We talked ourselves out of purchasing the house, because it was too far from our parents. We used distance to talk ourselves out of the blessing, but God is so faithful. We continued to look at homes, but nothing was clicking with us. Months later, the realtor called and informed us that the house was still waiting for us! That was unbelievable. Danny and I finally made a serious offer and stuck to it. God sees all things. As a result of our offer, my mother-in-law decided to purchase the house next door. She walked away when the builder changed the price.

Eleven years later, the same home came on the market again. My mother-in-law purchased the house this time, and she paid less than what the original seller required. God is always wise. He sees all the pieces of the puzzles and knows how and when to bring them together. My in-laws became our next-door neighbors and there were immediate changes. They were happy with the decision to live closer to us. Instead of a forty-minute drive, we now just walk across the lawn.

In obedience to the instruction from God, I was teaching my sons the word of God! This new arrangement was a time of transition for me, as I was not really in any specific ministry. I was in the School of the Holy Ghost where God was stretching and teaching me Himself. Tyler was about six and Miles four. I remembered them reading the children's Bible and fumbling over some of the words. Each Sunday, I taught them the Word of God. Our kitchen became the classroom. I taught them how to present the word of God.

I was committed to being obedient to God. I remembered when Father asked me to be his servant, that I resisted for some time. But the Word came to me, *"Where can I go from your Spirit? Where can I flee from your presence? If I go up to the heavens, you are there; if I make my bed in the depths, you are there. If I rise on the wings of the dawn, if I settle on the far side of the sea, even there your hand will guide me, your right hand will hold me fast."* I had no choice but to simply surrender and submit to his plans for my life. One Sunday, after breakfast, just before getting ready to teach the boys, the Spirit of the Lord whispered to me, "Why don't you call your in-laws and ask them if you can go over for Bible study?" I dismissed the idea, not because I did not want to obey, but because I did not know how my in-laws would react. I did not obey. My phone rang, it was my mother-in-law inviting me to come over and have Bible study at their home. Wow! We have been conducting Bible studies there since that time. We welcome additional families on each Sunday to study the word of God.

I have watched how God transitioned and transformed my in-laws by His word. They grasped the word of God and held on to the word without wavering. They knew of God, but God was becoming personal to them through His word. The meetings changed them. They recommitted their lives to God and are a source of strength, strong in faith. God is wise, orchestrated these different segments of our lives. God challenged me. He challenged my knowledge and understanding of Him. I have always been a "church girl," so not going to church, not being in a ministry, was outside of my comfort zone. Although I was not in ministry for many years, Gods' presence abides in my home. I will praise and honor Him always. What a Savior!

When my mother-in-law shared her news about the cancer, she was fully persuaded that God can do all things. She had already placed her trust and her confidence in him. We continued to rebuke the spirit of cancer, and we placed our trust in God our Healer. The time came for Ma to have the procedure, and we submitted her into the hands of God. The operation was successful, with results pending. The doctors indicated that she would be in the hospital for a few weeks. She was in the hospital for a few days. The doctors indicated that she would need a nurse upon her release. She did need nursing care. The doctors indicated that she would need chemotherapy. She did not have chemotherapy. When she returned for her follow-up check-up, there was no cancer. The doctors were amazed to see how quickly she was healing. Today, my mother-in-law is eighty-one years old and cancer-free. There is no one like God.

There is no power that is greater than the power of the Most High God. He lives and reigns forever! The enemy of our soul is persistent! He continued to pursue our family with the intent to steal, kill, and destroy using our health. A few months after receiving that healing victory, my mother-in-law's doctors informed her that her kidneys were severely damaged and failing. Her doctors wanted her to go on dialysis because her creatinine was high and over the cautionary levels. We agreed in faith and prayed. My mother-in-law has an unwavering faith. We prayed and held onto our faith. I prayed for healing, asking God to replace her damaged kidney. Her doctors were amazed at each visit because her creatinine levels were normal. There were instances when they went higher than expected, but we spoke the word of God, and God continued to give her a testimony.

If that was not enough, she started to develop ulcers on both of her legs. These wounds took over her legs from below her knees to before her ankles. The doctors told her that these wounds could take up to six months to heal. They were raw and painful, but God is not afraid of ulcers. We called on Jehovah Rapha, the Lord our Healer. We gave Him back His Word, reminding Him that healing is our legal right as children of the Most High God, because of the Blood of Jesus. Long before the six months that the doctors indicated, God dried up those legs. The doctors and nurses and everyone who was involved in her care were amazed.

Wave and wave of health problems persisted. I consider myself healthy, but I woke up with a piercing pain in my right side one day I was uncertain about what it was and presumed that it was my appendix. I went to my doctor, who informed me that I had a large fibroid on my right side. I was told that I would need to have surgery to remove it. I was in so much pain that I convinced myself that it had to be more than fibroids. I had my doctors conduct a scan, and the result was the same. It was what they estimated to be a ten-centimeters fibroid with smaller growing fibroids that could place me at risk. This finding was alarming as I did not have a history of fibroids or had any medical issues during my pregnancies.

During my time in the school of the Holy Spirit, I learnt about legal rights, and generational roots. The enemy's legal right to inflict me in this way was through the bloodline. My grandmother died at the age of 33 from fibroids. That door was still open, giving the enemy legal right to bring this disease through the bloodline.

I needed surgery. I consulted with several doctors and made a final decision. I was going to need a hysterectomy. This deeply saddened me. There were moments that I broke down in tears. I felt a profound loss, and although I was not planning on having any more children, I wanted my womb. Although this seemed to be the best solution forward, it was an amazingly emotional decision for me. I did not understand. I was hurt and started to grieve.

My gynecologist had no immediate openings in her schedule. I was in so much pain that she recommended me to a colleague who has a solid reputation in the medical community. I was able to get an immediate appointment for a consultation, but her surgery calendar was also full. According to her staff, there was a slim chance of any surgery dates becoming available immediately.

I asked God to choose the right doctor for me, and He did. I went in for a consultation and trusted God with the rest. This new doctor informed me that she was surprised that I was recommended to her. She stated that nothing about my situation was atypical, that her cases were extremely complex. One of the things that I observed about my new doctor was her attention to detail. She was meticulous in her note-taking. I recognized when taking notes her information was spelled correctly. That caught my attention.

After my consultation, I received a call from the doctors' office stating that a date became available. But God is wise! Doctors are limited in what they know, but God's knowledge is unlimited. If God sent me to this doctor there was a reason; for God makes no mistakes. I did not understand the purpose, I was in pain and needed help. I was told that my surgery should take about two hours, with the expectation to return home that same day. The plan was a laparoscopic procedure meaning going through the navel versus a cut on the stomach. This proceeding was easier and would have minimal healing time. However, I was told that a vertical incision, may be necessary.

While I was going through this process, my mother-in-law was still dealing with some health challenges. Her medical team suggested a fistula placement in her arm as a precaution for dialysis in case of emergency. She was hesitant at first but eventually capitulated to give my father-in-law peace of mind. Her surgery was scheduled for Thursday with a two-day hospital stay. Her surgery was successful, and she came home that Friday. I was scheduled for surgery on Monday. That Sunday morning, we received a call from Ma because her wound was bleeding profusely. We returned to the emergency room. The medical staff identified and corrected the problem, and she was able to return home that same day. She was in pain, but we were thankful to have the issue resolved.

It was Monday, and now my turn to go in for surgery. One cannot imagine the intense pressure on Danny and the rest of the family. We were dealing with so many different challenges at the same time. We prayed placing our family in the Lord's hand, and we trusted Him to keep us. I went into surgery at around 9:30 a.m. and came out at 8:00 p.m. that day. According to the doctor, the fibroid pressing on my right side had done some severe damages. The surgery moved from being laparoscopic to an incision made from my belly button to my pelvic bone. The fibroid pushed all my organs to my body's left side, and was growing around my spine. She had to carefully and meticulously remove the growth from my spine. Look at God! I spent the rest of the week in the hospital. I was in intense pain. It was three full months before my body felt normal.

I had a breakdown! I was in severe pain. My stomach was like a jigsaw puzzle with staples from one end to the other. My movements were painful because every part of my body hurt. As I laid in bed, I felt forsaken. Despair and hopelessness settled on me. Danny walked into the room and in that instant as our eyes met, my tears started. A floodgate opened, and all of my emotions which I buried so well was on full display. I cried uncontrollably. The tears were unstoppable. I was feeling helpless and abandoned. My faith had matured over time, but I was in a state of brokenness. I did not want to fight one more battle. I did not want to pray for one more thing. I was emotionally, physically, mentally, and spiritually depleted. I was exhausted from being tried and tested. At that moment, I did not care if I failed the tests. I wanted the exams to be over. I did not want to be strong for anyone else. I needed immediate reprieve.

Even amid uncertainty, I remembered that God is still God in our broken moments. Nothing in our lives takes Him by surprise. Our breakdowns are opportunities for God's strength to be magnified in our situations. Our testimonies are powerful when others can relate to the pain attached to our experiences, knowing that God still delivers. Danny and I were not going to walk away from God, but I wondered if God had abandoned us. King David wrote in Psalms 22, *"my God, my God, what hast thou forsaken me? Why are you far from saving me, so far from my cries of anguish? My God, I cry out by day, but you do not answer by night, but I find no rest."* David thought that his prayers were unheard. King David felt forsaken and forgotten. This scripture assured me that even those who are strong still need God's strength to undergo the hardships of life. Our lives often bring broken moments of utter desolation, but God reassures us that we are never alone. Baring our hearts to God teaches us confidence in His strength to carry us through. Jesus on the cross repeated the same scripture, *"My God, my God, what hast thou forsaken me?"* Jesus experienced deep pain. Pain that He did not deserve, but He endured for a sinful world. Jesus depended on the strength of His Father to carry Him through this dark hour. God is a reliable and trustworthy Shield and Banner to protect and comfort us in our moments of desperation.

I needed reassurance from God. I needed to know that God was with us, that what we were going through had a beginning, but also had an end. At that moment, the spirit of defeat had overtaken me. I was overwhelmed. The tears flowed. I did not ask God why all of this was happening; I just wanted to know when this would end. The surgery took a toll on my body. My body felt broken because of the incision and staples on my stomach. Additionally, I was struggling in my faith. My faith was weak. Danny and I held on to each other and cried out to God. We reminded ourselves of God's promises that are true and unfailing. We repeated His word back to Him, *"it is the same with my word. I send it out, and it always produces fruit. It will accomplish all I want it to, and it will proper where I send it."* Isaiah 55:11 We desperately needed God's promises to generate fruit in our lives, but these ongoing battles were exhausting. We understood the analogy of a seed dying in the soil to produce more, but we were tired. God's word which is seed, will always bring forth fruit. Wherever His word is planted there will always be prosperity, but the processing the fruit comes through brokenness. We knew that our lives would never be the same when we came out of these crippling circumstances. I encourage you in moments of desperation, no matter the struggles you are going through, God knows what is best for us. He knows how to manage the intensity of the fires we walk through in our lives. God our Father is trustworthy and completely reliable. I needed that moment of breakdown. I was strong for everyone in the family, but God wanted to remind me that in my weakness, His strength is made perfect in my life. Eventually, I dried my tears, and like David, we encouraged ourselves in the Lord.

As this chapter ends, it does not close our story. As a family, we continue to trust in the Lord with all of our hearts. I cannot tell you what our future holds, but I can let you know that as a family we have seen the hands of God in operation in our lives. It takes courage to live a life that pleases God. It takes courage to stand when it appears every fiery dart is being released at you. It takes courage to be different, and it takes extraordinary courage to stay in the fire of God. The fire of God are the tests, difficulties, hard times, and challenging periods that we endure in our life. To be in that kind of fire takes grace that only God can give. Only the grace and favor of God can bring us out of life's difficulties without allowing others to smell the hell that we have experienced. My encouragement to you is that if God has brought you into it—whatever your it is—He is going to bring you through it. Today I am looking forward to full restoration of all the things that has been stolen from us. God remains faithful.

CHAPTER 7

MY PRAYER OF THANKSGIVING

Father, I adore you! I repent for every sin of commission and omission. I repent where I have spoken foolishly and carelessly. I repent where I have grumbled and complained about the process. I repent for every foolish action and careless deed. Father, I apply the blood of Jesus over my life. I thank you for the covenant that I have because of the blood of Jesus. Today I will trust you. I love you, and I will wait for you.

Father, I thank you for placing my family in these unusual seasons. I do not understand, but I trust you. I know that what we have come through was You pruning and preparing us for the seasons ahead. You are strategically positioning us. I thank you that Esther found favor because she was obedient to You and submissive to the process, so too my family and I will confidently submit to the process and continue to obey you, in Jesus name. I am excited about what you are doing! I thank you for being with us in the process. Father, I may not have always enjoyed every part of the process, but I thank you for allowing us to go through the fire. I thank you that even those times when I could not feel You; when I turn to the left and the right and could not hear You, our faith was still persistent. I thank you that even when the tests were challenging, and our flesh screamed no, that our spirit said, "nevertheless not our will but thy will be done." Amen.

I thank you Father, that we are high above thrones, high above powers, high above principalities, high above authorities, and things visible and invisible. Amen. I thank you for the fresh breath of God that is breathing over us. I thank you Father, for all the things that

You are to us. You are our Father, our Healer, our Defender, our Provider and our God; I love you! Teach us Father, to love you more. Teach us to wait for you. Teach us to honor you with our life in Jesus name. Amen. Joshua 11 declares that Joshua did what he was told. I also want it to be said of me and my house that we did what we were told. Grant unto us an obedient heart, in Jesus name I pray. Amen.

BLESSED BEYOND MEASURE

In this final chapter, I want to remind you that God loves to bless his children. God is a giver, and He is a giver of good gifts. His Word declares in Mathew 7:11, *"If you, then, though you are evil, know how to give good gifts to your children, how much more will your Father in heaven give good gifts to those who ask him!"* God's love is beyond comprehension. We cannot measure God's love. This love is inconceivable and impenetrable. This is the love that God has for us. It is a perfect love! An enduring love! A passionate love! A love that penetrate the hearts of the vilest of sinner. A love that does not condemn! A love that far exceeds the love of parents and grandparents. A love that is richer and sweeter than spouses have for each other. It is from this heart of pure, sweet, and perfect love that God delights in blessing his children.

Our family believes God for full and complete restoration of what was lost over the past five years and beyond. We are asking God to restore to us, the blessings, gifts and talents stolen from previous generations. It is time to stand in our places of prayer and ask for full restitution of what has been stolen from us and the generations before us. We need to be a people that enjoy such deep intimacy with our Heavenly Father that according to His Word, in Hebrews 4:16 *"Let us, therefore, **come boldly** unto the **throne** of his **grace**, that we may obtain mercy and find **grace** to help in time of need."* We approach His Presence already knowing that He loves blessing us. We remain grateful for how God manifested His love and faithfulness to us during this time. Here are two examples.

One of the blessings that we enjoy as a family is taking vacations. My husband loves to travel, and as a result, we are privileged to travel several times a year. Our vacations do not always have to be travel abroad, but a well-planned road trip to another state or country meets that need. In 2014, going into the second year of unemployment, I recognized that the family was tired and needed a change of scenery. I asked God for a family vacation. It was a request between God as my Father and me as his daughter. I did not know how God was going to make this happen, but my role as a child of God was to simply ask, trust, and allow Him to be God.

Shortly after, I had a conversation with my mother. Now my mother knew that Danny was not working but I did not share the depths of what we were going through. I did not feel the unction to do so. I felt that God needed us to completely depend on Him. We placed our trust in God and stood on His word. My mother stated that she wanted to return to Montserrat, our island home, for a visit and asked me to join her. I informed her that I would not able to, as it would be not be wise for me to leave Danny. Danny was in a vulnerable place. I knew there were days that it was my faith that carried him through. I was not going to leave him behind. We changed the topic to speak about other things, and I soon forgot about the conversation. A few days later, my mother called and stated that she had given some thought to our conversation about visiting our island home, and she wanted to take my entire family to Montserrat for vacation.

My family and I went to Montserrat for three weeks that year. God heard and answered my prayer for a family vacation. I am reminded of the story of Abram in Genesis 15. In this story, God made a unilateral covenant. This covenant depended on God alone to bring it to pass. Abram was not able to seal the covenant because Abram fell into a deep sleep, so the covenant was sealed by God Himself. Hebrews 6:13–18. God is a covenant-keeping God. God keeps his promises. When God gives you a promise, He fulfills all of them in His time. God is faithful.

I allowed my teenage son to use my car to drive back and forth to school. The car was older and had recently started to experience problems. We took it to the mechanic and patched it up to keep it going, but even the mechanic was not very hopeful that it would last much longer. I continued to pray, trusting and believing God to protect us. During my daybreak prayer time one morning, I felt an urgent need to pray specifically For the safety of my sons. I also told God that we needed two cars and asked Him to provide them. Later that morning, we received a frantic call from Tyler. The car stopped on the highway. The amazing miracle is that on a busy highway during rush hour, the sudden stop did not cause an accident. Tyler put on the hazard lights, and waited a few minutes to start the car. The car started and he took the exit and was able to call us from a parking lot. God protects His children.

God gave us another miracle that day. We arrived at the parking lot where our car was parked and called a tow truck company. Our mechanic was one hour away. Tow companies make their money because they charge according to distance. For this particular distance, the cost was two hundred and fifty dollars, but that day, God favored us, and we paid eighty dollars. The mechanic told us that the car was not worth fixing. We had recently experienced this type of trouble with Danny's car. We were exhausted from hardship. The enemy was using repeated problems to tire us, but we were grateful for Gods' intervention in our family even though we were now down to one vehicle. For weeks we struggled with one car, getting the boys to school, and Danny to work.

Danny worked one hour away in the opposite direction from where the boys attended school. The reality of what we were dealing with was intense. Our credit was damaged, and we had absolutely no extra money. We were living paycheck to paycheck. All we had was faith in God's ability to make a way. I kept hearing in my spirit I will do it for you if you go to the dealer. Eventually, we went to a car dealer about five minutes away from us. We used the old car as a trade-in and prayed that the car would make it to the dealer. While at the car dealers, with bad credit and all, I told the young man that we needed not only one but two cars. My husband was surprised that I made the request, but I was living in faith. My friends, we were approved, and later that week, we drove away with two cars! God is a Provider!

It does not matter what you are going through, God is in it with you! We must learn to trust God and take authority in those instances that we need to. God is truth. He will not allow us to fail and to be embarrassed. I encourage you to stay in His presence and watch him turn your life around! If you have not experienced His presence, I invite you to get to know Him. His invitation extends to all, and He patiently waits for you to run into His arms. He will protect you. He will keep you. He will provide for you. I cannot tell you that your life will be free of troubles, but I will tell you that our God will be with you and fight for you as He has and continues to do for my family and me.

I challenge you to make a firm determination to choose to serve the One True and Living God. It is true that our life may sometimes be interrupted, but having God as our constant companion and champion, we are winners!

ABOUT THE AUTHOR

Condase Weekes-Best was born and raised in Montserrat, West Indies, and currently resides in Massachusetts, with her husband Danny, and their two sons, Tyler and Miles. Her love for reading started at an early age. She is an avid reader of books across different genres and a prolific writer. *Our Life Interrupted* is her debut entrance as an author, that brings her love for God together with writing her personal experiences of faith and trust through life's difficulties.

Condase is an ordained minister, a Bible teacher, spiritual counselor, international speaker, who seeks to show Gods' love, grace, and faithfulness. She encourages, strengthens, and empowers the people of God to stand in faith and trust God in all things.

More information can be found at Condase.com.

CPSIA information can be obtained
at www.ICGtesting.com
Printed in the USA
BVHW030946270921
617615BV00009B/309/J

9 781098 043308